Praise for Skye Jethani's *With*

Made of the stuff of spiritual classics and presented in simple, contemporary terms, Skye Jethani does each of us a great service in calling us to reimagine the way we relate to God. We so readily fall prey to living out distortions and reductions to our Christian faith—with disastrous consequences. You and I are far more than sinners, consumers, managers, and servants. We are dearly loved by God and made for eternal communion with him. Everything looks different when we live life in response to God's love.

Paul Louis Metzger, PhD,
professor of Christian Theology & Theology of Culture, Multnomah Biblical
Seminary and author of The Gospel of John: When Love Comes to Town

Since I dove into *With*, I can't stop thinking about it. Skye Jethani's insights will change how you think about God . . . and you . . . and how the two of you relate.

Dr. Kara E. Powell,
executive director of the Fuller Youth Institute

It doesn't matter, as old theologians were rumored to argue, how many angels can dance on a pinhead. But it does matter which preposition governs your faith—*over, after, against, for, from, under, with*. Who knew what huge worlds turn on such tiny words? Who knew what theological riches were laced into the bones of grammar? Skye has done a great service to the church. In prose elegant and clear, with insights keen and deep, he shows how everything changes with just one word: *With*. It's a book I want my whole church to read.

Mark Buchanan,
author of Spiritual Rhythm

Who knew that a preposition had so much influence? Skye's book will challenge the way that you think about God and faith digging deep into our motivations and heart issues. You can't read this book and not see yourself and others differently!

Margaret Feinberg,
author of Scouting the Divine and Hungry for God

Cleverly using four prepositions—*under, over, from,* and *for*—Skye Jethani convincingly diagnoses the reigning paradigms of life, whether secular or religious, and shows how each one has captured some element of truth but in the end is deficient. Ultimately, they miss the most important thing—real communion with the living God. Thus utilizing one final preposition, *With*, he lays out what it really means to know and experience communion *with* God—a life of faith, hope, and love—the very things that we all desperately want and need. This is a helpful, encouraging, and inspiring book.

Jim Belcher,
author of Deep Church

This book will do for our generation what J.B. Phillips, in his classic *Your God is Too Small*, did for his. *With* reveals views of God that can't satisfy and opens up the possibility for exploring a life *with* God that more than satisfies.

Scot McKnight,
author of One.Life and The Blue Parakeet,
professor of theology and biblical studies at North Park University

There's a good reason why Skye is a senior editor at Leadership Journal . . . he writes with a stylish verve, real intelligence, and spiritual depth. Suggesting that the basic posture that you adopt toward God determines the quality, meaning, and direction of your life, *With* is designed to head readers in the right direction.

Alan Hirsch,
author of Untamed, TheForgottenWays.org

with

SKYE JETHANI

REIMAGINING THE WAY YOU RELATE TO GOD

with

THOMAS NELSON
Since 1798

NASHVILLE   DALLAS   MEXICO CITY   RIO DE JANEIRO

Published in Nashville, Tennessee, by Thomas Nelson. Thomas Nelson is a registered trademark of Thomas Nelson, Inc.

Published in association with Creative Trust Literary Group, 5141 Virginia Way, Suite 320, Brentwood, TN 37027.

Thomas Nelson, Inc., titles may be purchased in bulk for educational, business, fund-raising, or sales promotional use. For information, please e-mail SpecialMarkets@ThomasNelson.com.

Scripture quotations marked ESV are from THE ENGLISH STANDARD VERSION. © 2001 by Crossway Bibles, a division of Good News Publishers.

Scripture quotations marked NIV are from HOLY BIBLE: NEW INTERNATIONAL VERSION®. © 1973, 1978, 1984 by International Bible Society. Used by permission of Zondervan Publishing House. All rights reserved.

ISBN-13: 9781595553799

Page design by Mark L. Mabry

Library of Congress Control Number: 2011931594

Printed in the United States of America

20 21 LSC 40 39 38 37 36

For Amanda
"We love because he first loved us."

Contents

1

Life *After* Eden

The Shadows

Fifteen hundred years ago, the emperor of Rome built a tomb for his beloved sister. The small building was designed in the shape of a cross with a vaulted ceiling covered with mosaics of swirling stars in an indigo sky. The focal point of the mosaic ceiling was a depiction of Jesus the Good Shepherd surrounded by sheep in an emerald paradise.

The mausoleum of Galla Placidia still stands in Ravenna, Italy, and has been called by scholars "the earliest and best preserved of all mosaic monuments" and one of the "most artistically perfect." But visitors who have admired its mosaics in travel books and on postcards will be disappointed when they enter the mausoleum. The structure has only tiny windows, and what light does enter is usually blocked by a mass of tourists. The "most artistically perfect" mosaic monument, the inspiring vision of the Good Shepherd in a starry paradise, is hidden behind a veil of darkness.

But the impatient who leave the chapel will miss a stunning unveiling. With no advance notice, spotlights near the ceiling are turned on when a tourist finally manages to drop a coin into the small metal box along the wall. The lights illuminate the iridescent tiles of the mosaic but only for a few seconds. One visitor described the experience: "The lights come on. For a brief moment, the briefest of moments—the eye doesn't have time to take it all in, the eye casts about—the dull, hot darkness overhead becomes a starry sky, a dark-blue cupola with huge, shimmering stars that seem startlingly close. 'Ahhhhh!' comes the sound from below, and then the light goes out, and again there's darkness, darker even than before."[1]

The bright burst of illumination is repeated over and over again, divided by darkness of unpredictable length. Each time the lights come on, the visitors are given another glimpse of the world behind the shadows, and their eyes capture another element previously unseen—deer drinking from springs, garlands of fruit and leaves, Jesus gently reaching out to his sheep that look lovingly at their Shepherd. After seeing the mosaic, one visitor wrote: "I have never seen anything so sublime in my life! Makes you want to cry!"

Like the tourists in Ravenna, many come into Christian faith with great expectations. They have heard stories of jubilation and salvation, of the power to overcome this world and experience the divine in inexpressible ways. But once inside the ancient halls of Christianity many are disappointed. Where is the light, where is the illumination? Our hearts seek God and the goodness, beauty, justice, and peace we've been told he provides, but he often remains hidden behind the shadow cast by an evil world.

My concern is that we are inoculating an entire generation to the Christian faith. Many come with a holy desire to know God, to experience his presence in their lives, to be cared for like sheep entrusted to a meek and gentle shepherd. But this is not what they see or experience. In fact, they may leave the church without ever seeing a beautiful and enthralling vision of LIFE WITH GOD. The lights are never turned on to reveal the beauty that is present just behind the shadows. Instead they are offered a substitute form of Christianity, one that cannot break through the shadows and that never really satisfies the deepest longings of their souls.

When their experience of faith leaves them disappointed, they may falsely conclude that Christianity has failed. In reality, to quote G. K. Chesterton, "The Christian ideal has not been tried and found wanting; it has been found difficult and left untried."[2] Or perhaps it might be more accurately said of our time that Christianity has not been presented and therefore has been left untried. The result is a generation disaffected and inoculated to the true Christian message.

But there are moments, unexpected and undeserved, when a coin is dropped and our vision is transformed by a bright burst of light. It may only be a brief glimpse, but in those moments we see the world behind the shadows, we see an entirely different way of relating to God, and we long for more.

The Postures

Unfortunately a great many people have settled for a darker existence, one under a shadow in which they relate to God in a

3

way that leaves them discontent. Consider the following examples of four people I encountered. All identified themselves as Christians, most had significant church backgrounds, but they each related to God in a different way.

○

I had not met Joel before he came to my office for what he called "spiritual advice." A middle-aged man with some success at business, Joel described himself as a Christian with a weakness for alcohol, women, and gambling—the latter being the reason for his visit. A bad run of bets was now jeopardizing his business.

"I'm sorry for your troubles, Joel," I said, "but I'm not sure why you've come to see me."

"I don't go to church," Joel said, "but I know what's right and wrong. I'm concerned that God isn't going to bless my business because of what I've done. I want to make things right with him. I can't afford to have my partners and God against me."

○

Mark was a very well-read man. He devoured every business leadership book he could find, but he wasn't a business leader. Mark was a pastor. We met at a ministry conference and shared lunch together.

"The problem with most pastors," Mark began, "is that they think they're immune to market forces. They don't understand the basic principles on which every organization rises or falls. They just don't teach that stuff in seminary.

"I can't stand all the spiritualizing that goes on at these ministry conferences. We're just coming up with excuses for being bad leaders—for not doing more. Do you think the managers of Walmart sit around and contemplate? Why do people expect us to sit around and pray all the time? I'm not going to let my church atrophy like so many others."

◯

Rebecca was a senior at a respected Christian college. With graduation just months away, she was wrestling with what she would do next.

"I've always dreamed of going to medical school," she said. "And I've got the grades to probably get in, but I'm just not sure I should do it."

"Why not?" I asked. "What's holding you back?"

"I'm not sure that's what God wants me to do. I mean, does the world really need another cardiologist? I want my life to matter more than that. I want to do something *really* significant."

"Like what?"

"Like be a missionary," she said. "Maybe in order to serve him, God wants me to sacrifice my dream of becoming a doctor. I just don't want to reach the end and feel that I missed out on a more significant life."

◯

"I don't understand what I did wrong," Karen said through her tears. "I tried my best to raise him according to the Bible."

Karen's teenage son was struggling with severe depression

and coping in unhealthy ways. His drug use only exacerbated the problem and led to more destructive behaviors.

"It isn't supposed to happen this way," she said, with equal doses of anger and pain. "We have always honored God in our home. We have always done what's right. We raised our kids God's way—on biblical principles. There's even a verse from Proverbs framed and hanging in our house: *Raise up a child in the way he should go, and when he is old he will not depart from it.* Why is God punishing us?"

○

Joel, Mark, Rebecca, and Karen represent the four ways most people relate to God. And like the tourists trapped in the dark and smelly confines of the Galla Placidia, most people are ultimately unsatisfied with these four approaches.

Life *From* God

Joel, the fast-living businessman, sought to use God to bless his business. He embodies the posture of LIFE FROM GOD. People in this category want God's blessings and gifts, but they are not particularly interested in God himself.

Life *Over* God

Mark, the savvy pastor with a focus on organizational principles rather than on prayer, didn't have much space in his life or ministry for God. This is the LIFE OVER GOD posture. The mystery and wonder of the world is lost as God is abandoned in favor of proven formulas and controllable outcomes.

Life *For* God

Rebecca, the graduating senior dreaming of medical school, was primarily concerned with how to best serve God. This most celebrated of religious postures is LIFE FOR GOD. The most significant life, it believes, is the one expended accomplishing great things in God's service.

Life *Under* God

Karen, the distraught mother who tried to raise her son "by the book," was upset when God did not uphold his end of the deal. The LIFE UNDER GOD posture sees God in simple cause-and-effect terms—we obey his commands and he blesses our lives, our families, our nation. Our primary role is to determine what he approves (or disapproves) and work vigilantly to remain within those boundaries.

Whenever I encounter new people, either in the church context or outside it, I'm usually trying to determine which posture best captures how they relate to God. A casual conversation about their life and faith and a few simple questions is usually enough to uncover their assumptions.

- Seatmate on a cross-country flight: "I really don't think much about God." Analysis: LIFE OVER GOD.

- Neighbor at the local farmer's market on Saturday morning: "If we can just stop these liberal judges, God will bless our country again." Analysis: LIFE UNDER GOD.

- Visitor at the church: "Every morning I wake up and pray for God to expand my territory. And he has!" Analysis: LIFE FROM GOD.

- Pastor talking about his congregation: "They're just lazy. What they need is some motivational preaching so they'll share their faith with their neighbors." Analysis: LIFE FOR GOD.

As Western culture becomes increasingly secular and "post-Christian," I find many more people unconcerned about God. They give little thought to how God's presence could or should influence their lives, and that's assuming they believe he exists at all. Many people in the secular West live *over* God.

But we must not exaggerate the secularization and post-God posture of the world today. Despite the rise of so-called "new atheism," there are still wars being fought because of religion in the twenty-first century, and traditional religious values dominate many communities even in Western societies. Adherence to faith rituals (or superstitions, depending on one's point of view) remains very popular today. Living *under* God's expectations is still important to many people. In fact, many of our cultural conflicts can be attributed to people living *under* God, seeking to impose their values on those who would rather live *over* him.

At the same time, a rapidly growing segment of people are seeking to use God for their personal benefit and profit. Some of the largest congregations in the United States and elsewhere are predicated on the LIFE FROM GOD posture, as are some of the best-selling Christian books. With so many traumas within families and now the turbulent economy, people are turning to God and his representatives for solutions. In many cases they don't actually desire God, just his supernatural help. Sometimes it is called consumer Christianity, the prosperity gospel, or health-and-wealth preaching. In each case people are looking to God as a cosmic therapist or divine butler. He's what one friend has called the WD-40/Duck Tape combo pack—all you need to fix just about anything.

What I find most among my peers in Christian ministry is a highly activist form of faith. Whether by fighting poverty, growing the church, or engaging politics, we tend to find purpose and meaning through what we do *for* God and his kingdom. The LIFE FOR GOD posture is highly celebrated and those capable of accomplishing the most receive great accolades and admiration.

Recognizing these four postures of life helps us makes sense of the church's work. Much of the church's activity is spent trying to move people from one of these four postures to another. For example, we try to convince a generally irreligious person living *over* God to care more about God's values and commands and to begin living *under* his rule. We don't push this simply to be dogmatic or intrusive, although at times that may be how it is received. Rather we believe that LIFE UNDER GOD is both more rewarding and blessed.

Some churches have made it their explicit mission to transform religious consumers into fully devoted followers of Christ. In other words they want people to stop simply living *from* God and start living *for* him. This shift is usually measured by a person's participation in church activities, charitable giving, service to others, and engagement in both local and international missions. We try to convince them to do less for themselves and more for God and others. A particularly successful shift from living *from* God to living *for* him occurs when a person leaves her chosen profession and enters "full-time Christian ministry."

Such stories are infrequent but highly publicized in faith communities.

A brief reflection on my own journey of faith reveals seasons in which I have occupied each of the four postures. I have lived OVER, UNDER, FROM, and FOR GOD. And when I think about my years in Christian ministry, I must admit that my efforts were largely focused on transferring people from one posture to another with mixed results. Sermons were written and preached, programs designed and launched, groups prepared and assembled, budgets created and tracked—all with the goal of moving people *over* God to *under* him and convincing others to start living *for* God and not just *from* him.

The Students

A few years ago I began to seriously question the four popular postures of the religious life. I knew LIFE OVER GOD was ultimately unsatisfying, and I wrote an entire book about the fallacy of consumer Christianity[3] and the emptiness of simply seeking a LIFE FROM GOD. But a more honest exploration of both LIFE UNDER and FOR GOD uncovered more disturbing things. My Christian tradition had taught me that obeying God's commands and being devoted to his work in the world was the prescription for joy, peace, contentment, and fulfillment, and this is what I had been teaching others. But after a decade in ministry, the evidence, within and around me, was failing to verify this assumption.

I could not explain why many of the people accomplishing the most for God seemed to reflect his character the least.

Rather than being marked by peace, patience, kindness, gentleness, and love, many of them were anxious, impatient, rude, aggressive, and sometimes even spiteful. This was not universally the case, I certainly know godly men and women in ministry, but the lack of godliness among church leaders was far more common than I was comfortable with. And I saw these same disturbing traits within me as I gave myself over to the work of God and ministry. Simply put, living *for* God was proving to be detrimental for my soul.

Similarly, there is an eerie correlation between meanness and how absolutely certain a person is about their beliefs. I'm not advocating agnosticism, but humility is in short supply among those seeking to perfectly demarcate truth and error, righteousness and wickedness, as they pursue a LIFE UNDER GOD. Those who pride themselves on their reverent submission to God's truth are strangely reluctant to submit to anyone else. The resulting conflict and animosity within Christian communities is difficult to reconcile with Jesus, who declared that the world would know we are his people by our love.[4]

My discomfort with the popular categories advocated by the church reached a tipping point a few years ago when I began mentoring a number of college students. Most of these very intelligent men and women had grown up in Christian homes. They had significant church involvement in their backgrounds, and some had even lived with missionary parents overseas. They knew the Bible better than most, and they could engage in meaningful theological and cultural discussions. I truly enjoyed my time with them.

But when I started exploring their personal communion with Christ, their practices of prayer, their understanding of sin, and how they related to God, I was dismayed. My questions were incomprehensible to some of the students. "What do you mean, how am I experiencing God?" one asked. Others admitted never being taught how to pray apart from the perfunctory grace before meals and bedtime. Most could not identify any time of meaningful transcendence or moments of peace or joy in God's presence. They often gauged the quality of their faith on one measure alone—how well they controlled their sexual desires.

Language about having a "personal relationship with Jesus Christ" has become cliché in many evangelical communities, including the Christian colleges most of these students attended. And yet when I scratched beneath the surface and used less familiar language to determine what their relationship with Christ actually looked like, most of the students fell silent. Many spoke about God as a theological reality, a sterile calculation, or the way an office worker at a large corporation might speak about the CEO whose portrait hangs on the wall but whom he's never met. Admiration and respect were evident and even a dedication to service, but personal knowledge of God was largely absent.

The students fell into the same four postures of religious life as most other people. Quite a few spoke about their desire to live *for* God and serve him in the world. Others, particularly those with theological acumen, lived *under* God by seeking definitive understanding of his laws and expectations. A handful used God for personal gain or relational assistance. They needed his help finding a spouse and securing "a ring by spring." They pursued a LIFE FROM GOD. And after a less than positive childhood immersed in the Christian subculture, some were ready to walk away from faith and live *over* God. These were the fully inoculated ones—the students who had waited all their lives for a compelling vision of Christianity but saw only darkness instead. They were ready to leave the church, believing they had experienced what Christian faith had to offer, when in fact they had only been exposed to a form of faith that had no real power.

These college students shared with shocking honesty and transparency. They were searching for answers and still forming their identities, and in safe and confidential settings many expressed a nagging dissatisfaction with their faith even while trying to follow it. They were stumbling in the darkness but had not given up. They were still hoping the lights would come on to illuminate the way. Their openness helped me see the problem more clearly than I had while serving in my church role. Through my time with these students, I became convinced that a great many of them had never really encountered the Christian message. They had spent their young lives trying to LIVE OVER, UNDER, FROM, or FOR GOD, and in most of their cases one of these postures had been advocated by their faith community. But none of them had been given a more beautiful vision. For these young people the possibility of a LIFE *with* GOD had never been illuminated.

The Intent

"In the beginning was the Word, and the Word was with God, and the Word was God. He was in the beginning *with* God."[5] This is how the apostle John described the beginning of all things. Before time or space, the preexistent God lived in eternal communion with *himself*. John introduced Jesus Christ, the "Word," as God, but also as existing before creation in unity *with* God.

The opening verse of John's gospel is one of many texts in the Scriptures that support the Christian belief in a trinitarian God. The Trinity, the notion of one eternal God existing in three persons (God the Father, God the Son, and God the Holy Spirit) is a foundational, and admittedly mind-twisting, doctrine of Christianity. But it is also where LIFE WITH GOD finds its origin. The Trinity reveals that we worship a relational and personal God. He is not an impersonal force as some Eastern philosophies teach, nor is he a disinterested creator as Enlightenment deism has advocated. The Christian God is a personal deity who exists in eternal community with himself.

God's relational nature is further revealed in his creative work. "Then God said, 'Let us make man in our image, after our likeness.'"[6] God established a garden in Eden where he placed the man and woman and where he walked *with* them.[7] God welcomed humanity into the eternal communion he had known since before time. We were created in his image so that we might live in relationship with him.

Eden was designed to be a collaborative environment where Creator and creatures worked *together* for a common goal. Eden is best understood as a base camp from which the man and woman were to extend God's garden to encompass the entire earth. They were intended to partner with God as his representatives and agents on the earth. The man and woman were instructed to "rule" over the earth on God's behalf and cultivate the order, beauty, and abundance of Eden in every corner of creation. This is the basis for the first command in the Bible: "fill the earth and subdue it."[8]

God's original intent for humanity to live and rule with him on the earth is also on display in the closing chapters of the Bible. The revelation given to the apostle John shows history's culmination:

> And I saw the holy city, new Jerusalem, coming down out of heaven from God . . . And I heard a loud voice from the throne saying, "Behold, the dwelling place of God is with man. He will dwell with them, and they will be his people, and God himself will be with them as their God."[9]

As in the garden in Genesis, the emphasis of John's revelation is that God and humanity will dwell together in relational unity. This is why God created us, and it is the end to which all of history is marching. Just as the first man and woman were intended to rule with God over his creation, that same purpose is reaffirmed in the book of Revelation:

> By your blood you ransomed people for God from every tribe and language and people and nation, and you have made them a kingdom and priests to our God, and they shall *reign* on the earth[10] . . . They will need no light of lamp or sun, for the Lord God will be their light, and they will *reign* forever and ever.[11]

If the Bible were the script for a play, both the opening scene and the final act of this drama would focus on God's desire to live and rule with his people. This impulse carries the drama from beginning to end. And yet the call to a life of intimate communion with God is largely absent today. It's as if we entered the theater late and left before the final curtain. As a result, we have a skewed understanding of the story. We've extracted one portion or another of the narrative and assumed it was representative of the entire story. This explains (in part) how we have come to exchange LIFE WITH GOD in favor of one OVER, UNDER, FROM, or FOR him. But our failure to embrace the whole story of Scripture doesn't entirely account for the error.

The Mountain

Failure to engage the whole drama of Scripture, including the opening and closing scenes, may partially explain why we have little vision for a LIFE WITH GOD. But we must also recognize that we live neither in the garden of Eden nor in the New Jerusalem. Our lives, and all recorded history, exist between these two paradises. And while the scenes in Genesis and Revelation show a world of beauty, order, and life-giving abundance, such things are difficult to find in our experience. We live in a world after Eden, a world marked by suffering, a world under a shadow.

Fear and suffering are the universal human experience, and every religion is an attempt to overcome this condition. It has become very popular to minimize the distinctive qualities in each religion by saying that "all religions lead to the same destination." The image of a mountain with many paths leading to the same summit is frequently used. According to this metaphor, each faith tradition has a different starting point and path but one needn't worry—they all converge at the top. Invariably such conversations involve platitudes about "loving others" and "doing good." Not only does this view fail to honor each religion's teachings, culture, and history of formation, but it seriously misses the common human longing from which all religions emerge.

A NOTE ABOUT ILLUSTRATIONS: Throughout the book you will encounter simple drawings that illustrate the key concepts in each chapter. I created these myself with just a marker and frequently use them when trying to communicate spiritual truths to our increasingly visual culture. I've found these doodles to be equally useful on a whiteboard in large group settings and on a napkin while having lunch with a friend. I've included them here to help you learn and so that you might share the ideas in a simple way with others.

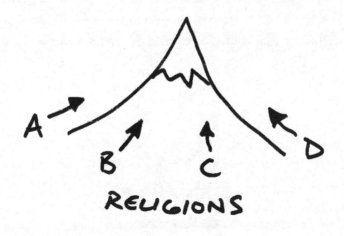

RELIGIONS

A more accurate image would invert the metaphorical mountain and place the point at the bottom to illustrate the shared starting place for all religion. We all share a world confused by chaos—we cannot predict what will befall us. We all share a world marred by ugliness—injustice and evil often appear to triumph. And we all share a world plagued by scarcity—we must strive to acquire what we need to survive. The greatest scarcity is life itself; we all live under the shadow of death. This shared reality, the nature of the world after Eden, is why we are all afraid. And to mitigate our fears, we all seek control over our world. If we can harness and control unpredictable forces, subdue our environment, and rule over our circumstances, then we can alleviate our fears—or so we believe.

Fear and control are the basis for all human religions. From this common beginning the paths diverge dramatically, splinter, multiply, and finally terminate in different places. But each one is an attempt to overcome suffering, fear, and death by exerting control over natural, and sometimes super-natural, forces.

This excursion into the philosophy of religion is important if we are to understand the four prominent postures of LIFE OVER, UNDER, FROM, and FOR GOD, which apply equally to religious paths other than Christianity. Each of these ways of relating to God is also an attempt to mitigate our fears through exerting control. But the problem, as we will explore in later chapters, is that they all fail to deliver on this promise. The reason, simply put, is that seeking control is not the solution to the human condition but is part of the problem. This, too, is revealed in a study of Genesis.

Although God created humanity to live and rule with him, the story in Genesis 3 reveals our reluctance to abide by this plan. Rather than living and ruling *with* God, the man and woman sought to be *apart from* him. This human quality is captured in a story familiar to many. A serpent deceived the man and woman into eating the fruit of a tree God had forbidden them to touch.

> The serpent said to the woman, "You will not surely die. For God knows that when you eat of it your eyes will be opened, and you will be like God, knowing good and evil." So when the woman saw that the tree was good for food, and that it was a delight to the eyes, and that the tree was to be desired to make one wise, she took of its fruit and ate, and she also gave some to her husband who was with her, and he ate.[12]

They did not take the fruit merely because it was appetizing or delicious. They ate because they wanted to "be like God." It was an act of rebellion—a coup of creature against Creator, a rejection of God and his plan to rule the earth with his people.

They no longer wanted to merely live *with* God. They wanted to *be* gods. They wanted control on their own terms.

The Scriptures and Christian tradition call this rebellious human desire for control apart from God *sin*. Our instinct, like all people, is to seek self-rule and a posture apart from God. This is why we have such difficulty grasping the call to live with him. And yet most of us retain some sense that God is important, that he must be factored into our lives in some way even if only to control him. But rather than engage in life-giving communion with him, we opt for one of the other four postures through which we try to manipulate, use, cajole, or appease him. Since Eden our human capacity to relate properly with God has been severely impaired. Like pilots in a fog with malfunctioning instruments, we cannot tell that we are flying upside down no matter how sincere our efforts at navigating may be. This is the effect of sin.

With this admittedly simple understanding of how sin has warped the way we relate to God, and the role of fear and control in human religion, let's return to the four characters I introduced at the opening of this chapter. Joel lived *from* God. He was afraid of losing his business. This fear brought him to my office in the hopes of "getting God back on his side." Joel wanted to use God to control the outcome of his business.

Mark lived *over* God. An ambitious young pastor with an admiration for leadership principles and organizational management, Mark feared that his church would atrophy like so many others. Rather than waste his time on "unproven" and unverifiable practices like prayer, he sought to control the growth of his ministry by employing "proven" principles.

Rebecca lived *for* God. The twenty-two-year-old's greatest

fear was insignificance. Unlike those who "wasted" their lives in what she deemed less important careers, Rebecca wanted her life to matter. She wanted to ensure significance and to control the outcome of her life by achieving great things for God's kingdom.

Karen lived *under* God. A caring mother and faithful churchgoer, she was afraid that her life and family would not be blessed. To ensure God's protection against the many dangers in the world, she made every effort to discern God's expectations and meet them. Karen tried to control God by her obedience.

What Joel, Mark, Rebecca, and Karen all lacked was a vision of LIFE WITH GOD. They had entered the Christian faith with great expectations; but without being given a higher and more beautiful vision, they settled for a less satisfying one. You may identify with one of their stories, and like them you may also not yet understand what a LIFE WITH GOD looks like. In the following chapters we will look more closely at each of the four popular postures, why each is so appealing, how each fails to deliver us from our fears, and how each risks inoculating us to the good news of Jesus Christ. But we will also start dropping coins into the box to turn on the lights and illuminate an alternative vision. Through brief glimpses of the world behind the shadows, you will begin to reimagine how you relate to God.

2

Life *Under* God

The Eunuchs

The bedroom door burst open and startled me from my sleep. My uncle entered the room with a large silver dish balanced on his head. The dish contained water, flowers, and what appeared to be a coconut on fire. Surrounding him was a flock of dancing and singing women—at least they appeared to be women. Once my tired eyes adjusted to the light and focused, I could see there was something odd about them. They were eunuchs—men castrated at a young age, dressed as women. They were clapping their hands and ringing chimes—their colorful saris twirling and glittering in the morning light. I thought I was dreaming. Where was the rabbit, the Mad Hatter, and the tea party?

I was nineteen years old and staying with relatives in Mumbai, India, to celebrate my cousin's wedding. Each day brought colorful new festivities and ceremonies. I like to consider myself culturally open-minded and tolerant of traditions other than my own, but this wake-up call by a desi drag parade was beyond bizarre. Eventually they left my bedroom and headed to the rest of the apartment. I got out of bed to find out what on earth was happening.

It was explained to me that in some Hindu traditions eunuchs are considered holy—genderless like God. Bands of eunuchs travel together looking for households celebrating marriages, births, or other milestones they might bless. Hearing of my cousin's wedding, they had arrived early in the morning to bless the union and the household. As the man of the house, my uncle became the central actor in the ceremony.

After the prayers, dancing, and burning of fresh produce was finished, the eunuchs stood at the door of the apartment, but they weren't nearly as joyful as when they had entered. They were quarreling with my uncle. Not speaking Hindi, I was again lost. "What's going on?" I asked a relative standing beside me.

"They're haggling over the payment," she said.

"Payment for what?" I asked.

"After they bless the house, the eunuchs expect to be paid. It's how they survive. They're angry because they don't think they've been paid enough yet. They're threatening to curse the marriage."

The argument lasted a few more minutes. I could see my uncle, a shrewd businessman with enterprises from New York to Hong Kong, becoming increasingly frustrated. But eventually the fear of a curse was too much to bear. He paid what they demanded. The gods were appeased. The marriage was blessed. The eunuchs were leaving. With the crisis averted I went back to bed.

The Bargain

The unusual scene in my relatives' apartment illustrates how a great many people understand the world. They believe their primary calling is to live under divine rules in order to avoid calamity. Some anthropologists and religious scholars see this sort of simple superstition as the basis for all human religion. They argue that appeasing deities is essentially what all religions do, that we've just become more elaborate and sophisticated in our approach. Let's strip away the convoluted theology and institutional trappings and take a look at religion in its simplest form.

Imagine a small community of ancient people in simple dwellings, living off the land. Their survival depended on forces far beyond their control. *Would the herds stick to their normal migration route this year? Would the rains come? Would the locusts destroy the crops? Would the fever spread?* Rather than explaining these forces of nature through science as later civilizations would, ancient peoples personified natural forces and linked them with deities. For the ancients the universe was not governed by *laws* but by *wills*—the wills of the gods. Spring did not arrive because the earth's axis shifted and more sunlight reached the northern hemisphere. Spring came because a god willed it to come. But the gods were capricious—their goodwill toward mortals and the sustaining of the natural order required sacrifices, rituals, and human obedience.

So religion became the way people participated in maintaining the universe and their own survival. Elaborate systems of superstition and ritual were constructed to make us believe that we are more than passive victims of chance. They convinced us that the blessings or curses of the gods did not occur randomly. Those who followed the rules, obeyed the ritual demands, and appeased the gods were rewarded with blessing. Punishment was reserved for the disobedient and the irreverent. Why didn't your fields produce as much this season as your neighbor's? Was it merely bad luck or an inferior method of farming? Not according to the LIFE UNDER GOD posture. You were less blessed because your sacrifices did not please the gods as much as your neighbor's. In this scenario religion is a way of understanding and controlling otherwise unpredictable forces, and with a sense of control people feel less afraid. At least that is the intent.

Today we may not offer a human sacrifice to ensure the sun will rise, but there are plenty of forces that remain beyond our control or understanding. *Will our business turn a profit this year? Will our children stay healthy? Will the investment pay a return? Will the Cubs make it to the postseason?* When faced with uncertainty, like the ancients we still refuse to believe that we are passive victims of chance. We want to believe that our actions can and do affect the world around us. In polytheistic or non-Western religions, like the Hinduism of my relatives, control is often sought through rituals. Offering prayers and sacrifices is a means of incurring the gods' favor.

Monotheism, the belief in a single creator God, first emerged around five thousand years ago and moved beyond the ritualism of more primitive religious systems. The monotheistic religions—Judaism, Christianity, and Islam—seek to win favor with and control God by combining rituals and morality. Live according to God's righteous expectations, we are told, and he will bless you and answer your prayers. It is a potent mix of pagan superstition and biblical morality.

LIFE UNDER GOD

Although widespread and deeply rooted in human history and civilization, this LIFE UNDER GOD approach has a number of significant shortcomings. Perhaps the greatest problem is that it only reinforces the rebellion of humanity we first saw in the story of Eden. If you recall, in Eden the man and woman were not content ruling *with* God, but instead wanted to be like God and assume a position of control. The irony of a LIFE UNDER GOD is that we are seeking to exert control *over* God through strict adherence to rituals and absolute obedience to moral codes. It is Eden's rebellion all over again. Through our obedience we put God into our debt and expect him to do our bidding in exchange for our worship and righteous behavior.

Consider the example of Steve Johnson, wide receiver for the Buffalo Bills. On November 28, 2010, the Bills faced off against their rival Pittsburgh Steelers. The Bills ultimately lost the game when Johnson dropped a pass in the end zone during overtime. After the game, via Twitter, he publicly blamed God for the loss. Johnson wrote: "I praise you 24/7!!! And this is how you do me!!! You expect me to learn from this??? How??? I'll never forget this!! Ever!!"[1]

The theology behind Johnson's tweet is a vivid example of the LIFE UNDER GOD posture. The football player has given God his worship ("I praise you 24/7"), and in exchange for this he expects to receive God's help on the field. When that help does not come, he blames God for failing to uphold his end of the deal. For Steve Johnson, and many others, religion is a means of seeking control over otherwise unpredictable events—in his case football games—by incurring divine favor. But notice that in this arrangement the creature (Steve Johnson) assumes a position of authority above the Creator (God).

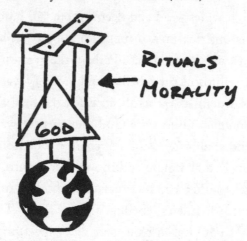

At first glance the LIFE UNDER GOD posture is incredibly appealing. It promises to take away our fears and garner divine blessing. But take a bite and you find you've been deceived. LIFE UNDER GOD cannot be a way of reestablishing a relationship with our Creator because it is actually an attempt to overthrow his rightful place. We may think of ourselves as devout, religious, humble, and even moral men and women of God. But in truth, like Judas, we are betraying our Lord with a kiss.

In addition, as Steve Johnson learned from his overtime defeat to the Steelers, the LIFE UNDER GOD approach is doomed to fail. As much as we might want to control God, history has proven that he is notoriously uncooperative. For every example of a prayer or ritual resulting in a positive outcome, there is one where the devout did not fare well. Consider the story told by Marcus Tullius Cicero about Diagoras, an ancient Greek who did not believe in the gods. He was shown the pictures of faithful worshipers who prayed and were later saved from a shipwreck. But Diagoras remained unconvinced. Instead he asked, "Where are the pictures of those who prayed, then drowned?"[2] Of course there were none. Dead people have a difficult time sharing their stories of the gods' unfaithfulness. By only selecting the stories of those for whom worship worked, an argument from silence is constructed to validate the LIFE UNDER GOD posture.

This still happens in Christian communities today. Many Christians are told that if they obey God's commands, if they worship him, give financially to the church, and abstain from immorality, then he will bless their lives. These pitches are validated by stories of people for whom the approach has worked. This message is particulary potent among adolescents. I recall sitting in a large gathering of teenagers while a notable Christian leader extolled the virtues of sexual abstinence before marriage. The preacher promised us everything from better grades and performance in sports, to outrageously satisfying sex once married, and all of it was tied together with assurances of God's blessing for our obedience. Testimonials were included from Christians about how God had blessed their marriages because "true love waits." Of course, no stories were shared by believers who had waited until marriage and were now divorced.

What happens when a young adult keeps his end of the bargain and it appears God fails to keep his? What happens when he worships him 24/7 and he still drops the pass in the end zone? What happens when her marriage isn't blissful, her grades are not good enough to get into the Ivy League school, or when life doesn't go as planned? Matt Chandler, a pastor in Texas, said that this is what's contributing to the "de-churched" phenomenon.[3] Young people raised within Christian communities are being taught a LIFE UNDER GOD view of the faith. And when God inevitably refuses to submit to our attempts at control via morality and ritual, they become cynical and abandon the church and in many cases the faith as well. The bargain turned out to be a scam.

The Crusaders

In chapter 1 we explored how fear and suffering are universal human experiences, and how all religion is an attempt to overcome them. LIFE UNDER GOD is no exception. This form of religion seeks to mitigate our fears by offering us control over the divine and therefore a degree of predictability in an otherwise dangerous and unpredictable universe. At least that is what LIFE UNDER GOD attempts. In reality, living under God does not reduce our fears, and a case can be made that it has actually made the world a more dangerous and fearful place.

The ancients tried to make sense of a seemingly random and chaotic universe by associating gods with the forces of nature and time. The sun is a giant ball of hydrogen and helium radiating energy generated by the force of gravity. People cannot control or argue with solar fusion. But a solar *god*, that is a different matter. If personalities and not immutable laws drive the universe, then human manipulation may be possible.

But rather than eliminating our fears, this approach merely transferred them. Believing that disaster, disease, and death are distributed by chance may not be comforting, but the thought of a vindictive god doling out pain and misfortune is downright terrifying. Following the rules and avoiding calamity is difficult enough in this world. Now I have to worry about getting on God's bad side as well? LIFE UNDER GOD does not solve our fear problem; it simply makes us afraid of God and not just his creation.

This is not to say God's moral instructions are bad. In both the Old and New Testaments it is clear that God issues his commands for our benefit and protection. He invites us to obey so "that it may go well with you."⁴ His instructions were designed to help us navigate through this world, but when morality slips into moralism, our fears are compounded rather than alleviated.

Moving beyond the individual, even more destructive things occur when the LIFE UNDER GOD posture dominates a community. If blessing or calamity is the result of obeying God's rules, then keeping everyone in line becomes the paramount mission of religious leaders. Faith gets reduced to dogmatism—adherence to strict moral codes and the enforcement of boundaries and rules. In such places the clergy function as divine police officers and cultural crusaders ensuring no one violates the Almighty's will, because it's not just the individual on the line, but the whole community.

Sometimes this is manifested in benign ways. In the early twentieth century, many fundamentalist Christians in the United States were forbidden from playing cards, dancing, or going to movies. Those who did were shunned and denounced as "worldly." But imposing strict religious expectation on communities can quickly escalate to more dangerous forms. In March 2010, the Palestinian Authority in Gaza ruled that men could no longer work in women's hair salons. The law conformed to conservative Islamic teaching. The order said, "Anyone who breaches this decision will be arrested and tried." In recent years men working in salons have been the targets of violent attacks.[5]

While it has become common to denounce some Islamic cultures for the cruel enforcement of religious law—the stoning of adulterers or forcing women to conceal their faces and forbidding them from driving—we should remember that Western cultures also have a sordid history. Not too long ago suspected witches were executed and heretics burned. But as Western societies became more secular they have frowned on imposing religious laws on citizens. This was most vividly evident in the founding of the United States and its Bill of Rights separating civil and religious authorities.

In secular societies, adherence to God's commands has become a matter of individual conscience, but this has put followers of traditional religions in a quandary. They believe God's blessings or curses are dictated by obedience to his commands, but they are no longer empowered to impose their religious convictions on the entire community. Instead they must pursue cultural crusades using channels in politics and popular culture to impress their values on the masses. The horrific events of September 11, 2001, reveal what happens when the LIFE UNDER GOD approach is taken outside the prescribed channels of a free society.

Three years before the attacks, the leaders of al-Qaeda issued a *fatwa* (an Islamic legal pronouncement) denouncing

the presence of American troops in the Arabian Peninsula—
"the holiest of places." Believing America was defying God's
will, al-Qaeda's declaration said,

> . . . in compliance with Allah's order, we issue the following
> fatwa to all Muslims: The ruling to kill the Americans and
> their allies—civilians and military—is an individual duty for
> every Muslim.[6]

When the United States failed to remove its forces from
Saudi Arabia, nineteen young men used airliners as guided mis-
siles to kill more than three thousand Americans in Manhattan,
Washington DC, and Pennsylvania. The terrorists believed
they were obeying God's will and would be rewarded for their
obedience.

But the perpetrators of the 9/11 attacks were not the only
ones displaying the tragic effects of the LIFE UNDER GOD posture. Shortly after the attacks, one prominent Christian leader
in the United States made the following statement:

> I really believe that the pagans, and the abortionists, and the
> feminists, and the gays and the lesbians who are actively try-
> ing to make that an alternative lifestyle, the ACLU, People
> For the American Way, all of them who have tried to secu-
> larize America. I point the finger in their face and say "you
> helped this happen."[7]

He went on to clarify his remarks by citing Scripture and
his belief that the immorality of the United States had led God
to remove his hand of protection from the country.

Sadly, these kinds of judgments are not uncommon when living *under* God is believed to be the essence of Christian faith. Other church leaders made similar remarks after Hurricane Katrina struck the Gulf Coast in 2005 and following the devastating 2010 earthquake in Haiti. Presumably, according to this logic, the way to prevent terrorist attacks and natural disasters (not to mention overtime losses to the Pittsburgh Steelers) is by earning the Almighty's protection through moral behavior, adherence to prayer, traditional family values, and frequent worship.

Events like 9/11, and the holy finger-pointing that followed, give ammunition to critics of religion like avowed atheist Christopher Hitchens. The *Vanity Fair* columnist and author of the best-selling book *God Is Not Great: How Religion Poisons Everything* makes a compelling case that religion adds to the fear in our world rather than reduces it. But an examination of Hitchens's critique of religion shows that he is primarily reacting to the LIFE UNDER GOD posture held by many who claim religious labels.

In a debate on the merits of religion with former British prime minister Tony Blair (a committed Roman Catholic), Hitchens asked, "Is it good for the world to worship a deity that takes sides in wars and human affairs, to appeal to our fear and to our guilt? Is it good for the world?"

Blair responded by noting how religion also motivates many people toward good and charitable actions. He gave the Northern Ireland peace accords as an example. Hitchens pounced on the statement:

It's very touching for Tony to say that he recently went to a meeting to bridge the religious divide in Northern Ireland, where does the religious divide come from? Four-hundred years and more in my own country of birth of people killing each other's children depending on what kind of Christian they were.

Hitchens went on to blame religion for blocking peace in the Middle East, for subjugating women in many societies, and for fueling the 1994 genocide in Rwanda—a country where 90 percent of the population claims to be Christian.

After the debate between Hitchens and Blair, the audience voted; 68 percent said that religion is a more destructive than benign force in the world.[8]

It is difficult to squabble with Christopher Hitchens's evidence that traditional religion fuels violence, bigotry, and oppression, and therefore adds to the fear and suffering in our world. (In chapter 3 we will explore why Hitchens's prescribed solution of atheism is equally flawed.) If LIFE UNDER GOD was intended to reduce our fears and provide greater control over our unpredictable world, it has proven to be an utter failure. Any way of relating to God predicated on fear and fighting for control cannot deliver us from what plagues humanity—namely, fear and fighting for control.

The Yoke

It may surprise some people, but at times Christopher Hitchens sounds a great deal like Jesus. Like Hitchens, Jesus frequently spoke out against the hypocrisy and harm inflicted by the religious system of his day. As one might expect, the LIFE UNDER

GOD posture dominated Jewish culture two thousand years ago. The popular belief about God followed a simple formula—God blessed the righteous and cursed the unrighteous. Obey his commandments, it was taught, and one could avoid disease, accumulate wealth, and find favor with God and men. The equation worked just as well in reverse. Those with material blessings were seen as righteous, and those who suffered did so because they were sinners.

This LIFE UNDER GOD formulation is clearly displayed in John 9. When Jesus encountered a blind man, his followers asked him, "Rabbi, who sinned, this man or his parents, that he was born blind?" In their view blindness was a curse, a judgment handed down from God in response to someone's disobedience. But Jesus quickly refuted their assumption. "It was not that this man sinned, or his parents, but that the works of God might be displayed in him."[9] He then restored the man's sight.

In another scene we see the opposite assumption on the part of Jesus' followers. After a very wealthy man declined an invitation to release his possessions and follow him, Jesus said, "How hard it is for the rich to enter the kingdom of God! Indeed, it is easier for a camel to go through the eye of a needle than for someone who is rich to enter the kingdom of God."[10] The statement astonished those who heard it. The popular belief was that God had blessed the rich—those possessing health, wealth, and comfort—for their righteous devotion. Being rich was tangible proof of God's approval. But Jesus declared the opposite—wealth can be a barrier to God and therefore not necessarily a blessing from him.

At every opportunity Jesus dismantled the LIFE UNDER GOD posture of his culture. Disobedience did not automatically mean calamity would befall you. And obeying the rules did not guarantee material blessing and avoiding hardship. But Jesus saved his harshest criticism for the religious leaders who promoted and benefited from the corrupt system.

Jesus finally broke out against the leaders (Matthew 23). He made two primary charges against them. First, "They tie up heavy burdens, hard to bear, and lay them on people's shoulders."[11] The LIFE UNDER GOD view puts its emphasis on appeasing God through behaviors—either in the form of rituals or morality. Formal religions, and those leading them, often create elaborate and arduous lists of requirements for their followers—the "heavy burdens" Jesus condemned. Trying to get everyone to follow the rules and live by divine expectations, as oppressive Islamic regimes and Christian fundamentalists attempt today, is not what God intends for his people. It's not what will set us free from fear and evil.

The list of requirements religious followers were expected to obey in ancient Israel was referred to as a "yoke." In contrast with the heavy burden other teachers placed on people's shoulders, Jesus said, "Come to me, all who labor and are heavy laden, and I will give you rest. Take my yoke upon you, and learn from me, for I am gentle and lowly in heart, and you will find rest for your souls. For my yoke is easy, and my burden is light."[12]

Jesus' second charge against the religious leaders was hypocrisy. Remember, the LIFE UNDER GOD posture is fixated on behaviors—following rituals and obeying commands. This way of relating to God places the emphasis on external and visible actions. *Did you give a sacrifice? Did you attend the church service? Did you eat the right foods and do you wear the right clothing?* But what LIFE UNDER GOD cannot do is look into a person's heart. Although one's behaviors might conform to expectations, inside you may still be consumed by hatred, greed, pride, lust, and deceit.

This is what Jesus saw in the religious leaders of Israel. He acknowledged that their external behaviors *looked* righteous, but internally they had missed what really mattered: "You tithe mint and dill and cumin, and have neglected the weightier matters of the law: justice and mercy and faithfulness."[13] Their lives epitomized the problem with the LIFE UNDER GOD approach— on the surface everything looks great, but dig any deeper and you end up holding your nose.

This was the very definition of hypocrisy: the outside does not match the inside. Jesus described these advocates of LIFE UNDER GOD with two additional unappealing metaphors. First, he said they were like dirty dishes. They cleaned the outside of the cup and plate so they appeared good, but inside they remained filthy—full of greed and self-indulgence.[14] And finally, he called them "whitewashed tombs." On the outside they were clean and beautiful "but within [were] full of dead people's bones."[15]

Tombs and dirty dishes are not what God had in mind for his people. Jesus modeled a different approach. As we've already seen, he announced that what he required—his "yoke"—was not burdensome. He did not expect people to perform arduous rituals or live under the constant threat of God's anger for their moral failures. And he did not teach that only those who reached a certain level of religiosity had access to God. In fact, Jesus displayed values deeply at odds with those of LIFE UNDER GOD. Chief among them was his unfiltered hospitality.

Jesus welcomed everyone, including those deemed unrighteous, to be with him. He was regularly seen in the homes of people believed to be on God's "naughty list," and he often shared his table with prostitutes and thieves. On multiple occasions the religious leaders questioned Jesus about this. "Why do you eat and drink with tax collectors and sinners?"[16] They were floored that a rabbi and prophet like Jesus would contaminate himself and risk incurring God's wrath by communing with such riffraff. Jesus also made a point of violating religious customs and rituals in order to show love and compassion toward the suffering. While the religious leaders sought obedience and conformity of behavior, Jesus sought to welcome people back into relationship with God. He inspired love and compassion, not simply sacrifice.

Through both his words and actions, Jesus revealed the bankruptcy of the LIFE UNDER GOD posture. It does not deliver us from fear. It cannot reconnect us with God. And in most cases it only burdens people under the weight of guilt, fear, and empty religiosity. The problem with the LIFE UNDER GOD posture can be summarized with the words of the prophet Isaiah, whom Jesus quoted while rebuking the religious authorities: "These people come near to me with their mouth and honor me with their lips, but their hearts are far from me. Their worship of me is based on merely human rules that have been taught."[17]

3

Life *Over* God

The Dream

In the last chapter we saw how traditional religion, LIFE UNDER GOD, has failed to deliver us from fear. Making matters worse, many of those driven to appease God and stridently follow what they believe are his commands have inflicted incalculable harm. They have used fear, guilt, and sometimes violence to force others to live under their religion's heavy yoke. This led atheist Christopher Hitchens to argue that the world would be a more peaceful and equitable place without belief in God. And he's not the only one.

In 1971, John Lennon released the song "Imagine." In the lyrics Lennon calls himself a "dreamer" who imagines a world without nations and without religion. Without these, he says, there would be "nothing to kill or die for." Once ideas about heaven, hell, and God are removed, it becomes possible to "imagine all the people living life in peace."

The song became an instant hit. And despite the many

brilliant tunes he wrote and performed with the Beatles, "Imagine" has become Lennon's most famous song. *Rolling Stone* even ranked it third on their list of "The 500 Greatest Songs of All Time."[1]

There are numerous reasons "Imagine" made such a profound mark on the culture. Beyond Lennon's beautiful melody and simple vocals, the song was released in a tumultuous time— the Vietnam War, the civil rights movement, the cold war, and the assassinations of John Kennedy, Martin Luther King Jr., and Robert Kennedy were all hanging like a cloud over a generation of young idealists. And then came John Lennon's murder in 1980. His tragic death added even more gravity to his dream.

In October 2010, a large crowd of Lennon's fans gathered to celebrate his seventieth birthday not far from the site of his slaying. They sang his songs and remembered his dream of a world without religion—a world at peace. They assembled at Lennon's memorial in New York's Central Park—a large circular mosaic with a single word inlaid at the center: IMAGINE.

Ironically, while Lennon's fans gathered to celebrate his dream of a world without religion, marked by unity and peace, the largest atheist organization in the country met in Los Angeles for a conference marked by schism and conflict. The Council for Secular Humanism met to deride Christians, Jews, and Muslims. Religious faith was called "nonsense" and "superstition," and adherents were described as "ignorant" and "stupid."[2]

But what got the attention of the *Los Angeles Times* was the heated conflict that erupted between two rival factions within the atheist movement. On one side were the "new atheists" who advocate open confrontation with religious believers. Rather than a live-and-let-live approach, they believe religion must be called out for the sham that it is. (Christopher Hitchens is one of new atheism's most visible leaders.)

On the other side are the "accommodationists." These moderate atheists don't believe direct confrontation with the religious is justified. They advocate partnering with religious people and institutions to advance issues of mutual concern.

The conference of "post-religious" leaders was hardly a utopian gathering of reason and thoughtful dialogue. The *LA Times* described it as tense and noted that the argument between the two factions was so contentious that it got "nearly physical."[3] Perhaps forgoing God and religion isn't a guaranteed recipe for peace as John Lennon had imagined.

Many people would like to believe that the problems plaguing our world could be solved if we simply put divisive ideas behind us, religion being chief among them, and then work toward a more harmonious future. This is what John Lennon sang about in "Imagine." It is also an apt definition of the LIFE OVER GOD posture—humanity living without God and free from the fearful superstition of religion. But this view ignores two critical things—human nature and history.

Václav Havel, the former president of the Czech Republic, was imprisoned for resisting the Communists in the 1970s and '80s. When he was released and elected president, Havel surprised many by being noticeably forgiving toward his political enemies. Some criticized him for this stance and misinterpreted it as weakness. But Havel reminded the Czech people that "the line between good and evil did not run clearly between 'them' and 'us,' but through each person."[4]

As we saw in the last chapter, people are capable of terrible things when fueled by a sense of divine imperative. But removing religious motivation does nothing to diminish our human capacity for evil. This is because, as Havel said, evil is not an externally constructed force or the product of religious doctrine. Evil runs through each human heart. Therefore, if we remove religion, that particular motivation for conflict may be gone, but people will surely find some other reason to fight and kill each other. Enslavement to sin is no less real in secular societies than in religious ones. It is our broken human nature, and history painfully affirms this fact.

Some of the most oppressive regimes of the twentieth century were constructed on the philosophical foundations of secular atheism. Precise numbers are difficult to determine, but in Stalin's Soviet Union, some estimate twenty million people were killed. Mao's Cultural Revolution in China resulted in sixty-five million deaths. And the Khmer Rouge decimated an entire generation, two million people, in Cambodia's killing fields just a few decades ago. The oppression continues in North Korea where at least two million have been killed.[5]

Many of the criticisms of LIFE UNDER GOD are justified, but LIFE OVER GOD fares no better. Secular humanism has no record of removing fear, fostering peace, or leading to a more just and verdant world. Advocates of atheism may dream of a better world without religion, but their solution forces us out of the frying pan and into the fire.

The Apple

My purpose is not to construct a philosophical or cultural argument against atheism. Others have done so in recent years in response to the "new atheists," and I feel no need to repeat their work. My concern is with those who claim Christian faith and even participate in a local church but actually have the same LIFE OVER GOD posture as atheists. I know this may sound odd, but there are many Christians whose understanding of faith has been shaped by the same cultural, historical, and philosophical forces that give rise to atheism. As a result, they practice a faith that has little room or need for God.

The contemporary shape of the LIFE OVER GOD posture might be traced back to a seemingly inconsequential event in 1666. Sir Isaac Newton, the English physicist, was contemplating the nature of the universe in his garden when he saw an apple fall from a tree. Newton wondered, Why must the apple always fall toward the earth? Why not sideways or upward?

The falling apple launched Newton's quest to define the law of gravity. Eventually Newton's work in physics, mathematics, and astronomy inaugurated a revolution in scientific thought called the Enlightenment.

The Enlightenment fundamentally changed the way people saw the cosmos and how they related to it. Imagine that Newton's apple represents the universe. The pre-Enlightenment belief was that if you peeled away the skin and cut through the flesh, at the core of the universe you would find divine will. The LIFE UNDER GOD view of traditional religions, as we explored in chapter 2, says that the universe is sustained by the mysterious will of the gods or God. In this posture, humans seek to mitigate their fears by controlling the God who controls the world, by manipulating him through rituals or morality.

But the scientific revolution and Enlightenment thinking presented a very different view of the universe. Cut into the apple and at the core one would not find divine will, they said, but natural law. The universe was not sustained by capricious deities but by predictable and rational principles. This view of the cosmos utterly changed our understanding of our place within it. The desire to control our environment and mitigate our fears no longer required appeasing God. Instead, the new view said the universe was like a machine, and our job was to understand how it operated and then leverage those principles to control it. Using mathematics and the scientific method, humans could discover the immutable laws that ruled everything from the motion of the planets to the origins of life.

It has taken hundreds of years for the implications of this new understanding of the universe to be worked out in practice, and in some underdeveloped parts of the world it is still difficult to see. But in most modern cultures it is clear that the Enlightenment view has eclipsed the traditional view of the world. For example, before the Enlightenment, illness sent people to religious leaders for prayer. They sought God's mercy through rituals and sacrifices. But today illness sends most people to the pharmacy for medicine. Science has explained why we become sick and has produced chemicals to restore our health. Fear still drives us to seek control, but this control is now achieved through science rather than superstition.

Post-Enlightenment cultures have pushed God out of the space he once occupied. Faith and religion have become marginalized and reserved for those few aspects of human existence science cannot (yet) explain and control. For some this new understanding of the universe has done more than marginalize God, it has eliminated him altogether. But despite the best-selling books and increased attention given to vocal atheists like Christopher Hitchens and Richard Dawkins, the vast majority of Americans still believe in God. A 2008 survey by the Pew Research Center found that only 1.6 percent of Americans are atheists.[6]

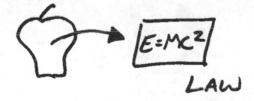

Although belief in God remains popular, most people's understanding of God and how to relate to him has been severely impacted by Enlightenment thought. In fact, recent sociological studies have concluded that most people in the United States do not hold a traditional or biblical view of God; most people unknowingly subscribe to a form of deism. Deism, unlike atheism, affirms that God exists and created the universe, but it believes he is now distant and relatively uninvolved in the matters of ordinary life. The watchmaker analogy is often used to describe deism: God constructed the cosmos and put all the required cogs and springs (natural laws) in place. Then he wound it up before stepping away. Now the universe runs automatically without requiring his direct involvement.

Whether it's atheism or deism, the practical implication is the same—God simply has no bearing on one's daily existence. And the fears and uncertainties that mark our human experience are dealt with the same way—by seeking control. LIFE UNDER GOD seeks control of the world through religion, by manipulating God through ritual or morality. LIFE OVER GOD dismisses this as irrational superstition and seeks control by

discovering how the world works and then directly implementing the right principles. LIFE OVER GOD effectively cuts out the middleman and gives us direct control over our lives.

Many battles in the so-called "culture wars" can be explained by the opposing worldviews of those in the *under* and *over* God camps. For example, scientific research has shown that teaching teenagers about safe sex and condom use reduces sexually transmitted diseases. In many communities, however, religious beliefs dictate that only sexual abstinence should be taught, despite evidence that "abstinence only" programs fail to reduce the number of sexually active teens.[7] The battle over sex education in public schools is often fought between those with a scientific worldview (LIFE OVER GOD) and those with a religious worldview (LIFE UNDER GOD). One values empirical evidence and the other biblical morality.

Or consider recent spats in the United States over displaying the Ten Commandments in government buildings. Secular thought (LIFE OVER GOD) sees natural law as the basis for civil authority. Religious conviction (LIFE UNDER GOD) sees law rooted in divine revelation. Whether the issue is sexual morality, prayer in schools, the definition of marriage, or what qualifies as art, the disagreements fall along predictable fault lines based on two very different ways of seeing the world and God's place in it.

But even among those who might consider themselves religious, the Enlightenment understanding of the world still holds great influence. Christians who might be on the front lines of the culture war, fighting for a traditional understanding of sexuality or law, may nonetheless manage their own lives and churches from the LIFE OVER GOD posture. We may not want to admit it, but like secularism, deism, or atheism, many popular forms of modern Christianity leave little room for God.

The Watchmaker

A few years ago my colleagues at *Leadership Journal* interviewed an influential church leader. Others throughout the world have copied the programs and processes of his church. During the interview he was asked, "What is distinctly spiritual about the kind of leadership you do?"

"There's nothing distinctly spiritual," he replied. "One of the criticisms I get is 'Your church is so corporate'. . . And I say, 'OK, you're right. Now, why is that a bad model?' A principle is a principle, and God created all the principles."[8]

His answer illustrates the degree to which Enlightenment thought has shaped our understanding of God and faith. The worldview behind his statement is the same as that held by deism—God has created the cosmos with certain knowable and immutable laws. Among them are the laws of gravity, the laws of thermodynamics, and the laws of mathematics. But modern people have expanded the list to include other areas of life such as leadership, relationships, and business. In order to function properly, our task is to discover these laws and translate them into applicable principles. In this view God is the law-writer, the principle-creator, the watchmaker.

The problem with the world, this view might argue, is that most people are not living by the right principles. They are trying to run a diesel truck on fruit juice—it just won't work. Rather than applying the principles of life derived from scientists, political leaders, or Oprah Winfrey, they should be living by God's principles. After all, as the Creator of all things, he knows what's best, right?

This understanding of God informs how many Christians engage the Bible. They believe the Scriptures are a divine instruction manual for life; a resource to be culled for principles that may then be applied to any challenge or dilemma. I've heard pastors quip that B-I-B-L-E stands for "**B**asic

Instructions **Before Leaving Earth**," and others have called it the "owner's manual" for a human being. We may chuckle at these cute metaphors for the Bible, but behind them is a very un-Christian understanding of God and ironically an unbiblical one rooted in Enlightenment thinking.

When the Bible is primarily seen as a depository of divine principles for life, it fundamentally changes the way we engage God and his Word. Rather than a vehicle for knowing God and fostering our communion with *him*, we search the Scriptures for applicable *principles* that we may employ to control our world and life. This is not Christianity; this is Christian deism. In other words, we actually replace a relationship with God for a relationship with the Bible. If one has the repair manual, why bother with the expense of a mechanic?

I realize that in Christian traditions holding a very high view of the Scriptures, like my own, it may sound as if I am downgrading the importance of the Bible. That is not the case. It is God's Word, inspired by him, and the authority for our faith and lives. Through it we discover who he is—and what greater gift can there be? And it does contain many useful and applicable principles for life and faith. But in our zeal to honor the importance of God's Word and extol its usefulness, we may unintentionally do the opposite. We may reduce the Bible from God's revelation of himself to merely a revelation of divine principles for life. And we are not the first to fall into this subtle trap.

The religious leaders in Jesus' time were expert students of the Scriptures. They had memorized the entire Hebrew Bible (the Old Testament). And they had parsed every command, extracted every principle, and delineated every instruction it contained. But their mastery of Scripture had not resulted in actually knowing God or recognizing him when he stood right in front of them. Jesus said to these leaders, "You search the Scriptures because you think that in them you have eternal life; and it is they that bear witness about me, yet you refuse to come to me that you may have life."[9]

This is the sinister shortcoming of the LIFE OVER GOD posture. It causes us to reduce faith to principles, divine laws, and applicable instructions: five steps to a more godly marriage, how to raise kids God's way, biblical laws of leadership, managing your finances with kingdom principles, etc. But discovering and applying these principles does not actually require a relationship with God. Instead, being a Christian simply means you have exchanged a worldly set of life principles for a new set taken from the Bible. But like an atheist or deist, the Christian deist can put these new principles into practice without God being involved. God can be set aside while we remain in control of our lives. He may be praised, thanked, and worshipped for giving us his wise precepts for life, but as with an absentee watchmaker, God's present participation is altogether optional.

The LIFE OVER GOD posture is particularly tempting in affluent, professional communities where people are accustomed to off-the-shelf solutions and self-help manuals. Their education and wealth mean they are used to being in control of their lives, and a huge publishing industry has ensured they maintain this illusion. Many best sellers are self-help books advocating principles to overcome nearly any problem. While proven formulas might be expected for losing weight or growing a vegetable garden, we tend to apply scientific certainty to even the more mysterious areas of life. Success can now be achieved by employing *The 7 Habits of Highly Successful People* and unruly kids can be tamed with *1-2-3 Magic: Effective Discipline for Children.* Perusing the shelves at the local bookstore can be a very comforting exercise. Knowing that there is a solution to any problem life throws at you provides a sense of control—it calms our fears. And if the answer cannot be found at the bookstore, we know there is always the pharmacy down the street.

Those of us used to being in control carry this same expectation into our religious lives. We approach the Bible with an eye toward three-steps-to-the-solution. We see this in contemporary preaching with its emphasis on practical application, and it also spills into the seven-billion-dollar Christian publishing industry. Consider the wildly popular book *Jesus, CEO* by Laurie Beth Jones. She studied the New Testament to decipher how Jesus managed to lead so effectively. Jones reduced Christ's management style down to three core principles: self-mastery, action, and relationship skills. She called these Jesus' "Omega management style" and asserted that they can be applied with equal effectiveness in any area of leadership—business, government, or religion. "Anyone who practices these spiritual principles," she wrote, "is bound to experience success. In fact, the study and application of spiritual principles comes with success guaranteed."[10]

Jesus, CEO advocates leading like Jesus without actually needing Jesus to be involved. He has been replaced with a set of principles—simple as 1-2-3. This same trend is evident in many other areas of contemporary Christian teaching. It is now possible to have a "Christian" marriage, a "Christian" business, and even a "Christian" nation without Christ actually being present. The fact that the principles are derived from the Bible is enough to convince us that they are—and therefore we are—indeed Christian.

The LIFE OVER GOD posture's emphasis on working principles may be appealing because it is far more predictable and manageable than an actual relationship with God. Relationships, whether human or divine, are messy, time consuming, and often uncontrollable. But principles are comprehensible and clinical. Perhaps this explains why a 2005 study found that only 3 percent of pastors listed prayer as a priority in their ministry.[11] If he's already given you the watch, why bother maintaining a relationship with the watchmaker?

The Staff

Although the Enlightenment provided a new scientific and philosophical basis for the LIFE OVER GOD posture, there is nothing essentially new about it. The original rebellion of humanity in Eden was an attempt to cut God out of the picture and take control for ourselves. And this same tendency is represented throughout the Scriptures. Sometimes the desire to live *over* God is fueled by arrogant pride, but just as often it is birthed out of fear. Consider the story of Moses in Numbers 20.

The Israelites had been slaves in Egypt for four centuries. Seeing their bondage and hearing their cries, the Lord sent Moses—an eighty-year-old ex-offender turned livestock engineer—to rescue his people from the oppression of Pharaoh. Throughout the dramatic rescue operation, God regularly demonstrated his power through Moses' staff. It became a snake before Pharaoh's magicians. Moses lifted up his staff to call down the plagues on Egypt. He touched the waters of the Nile with it and turned the river to blood. And he famously lifted his staff to part the sea so the Israelites could leave Egypt on dry land.

But leaving Egypt was only part of the story. In the wilderness of Sinai, the people faced other obstacles, not the least of which was a severe lack of water. On one occasion God told Moses to strike a rock with his staff. He obeyed and clean water miraculously flowed out.[12] A very similar scene unfolded again in Numbers 20. The people were angry with Moses for leading them into an "evil place" without food or water. Even the oppression of Egypt was better than this, they said.

Moses, as he had done so many times before, turned to God for help. The Lord instructed the beleaguered leader to "tell the rock before their eyes to yield its water. So you shall bring water out of the rock for them."[13] But something happened to Moses between communing with God and assembling the people before the rock. Rather than obeying the Lord and speaking to the rock, Moses struck the rock with his staff. He disobeyed God. But why?

Consider the scene again. Moses was between a rock and a hard place—literally. A furious mob of starving and thirsty people was ready to riot if he did not solve the problem. His neck was on the line. He needed a guaranteed solution, something he could count on, a way of supplying water that could not possibly fail. So Moses turned to what had always worked in the past—his staff. Fear and the need to control the outcome led Moses to disregard his communion with God and instead put his trust in a proven formula. He put his faith in the watch rather than in the watchmaker.

Moses paid a heavy price for allowing his fear of the people to overshadow his faith in God. The Lord forbid him to enter the promised land—the country promised to the Israelites and that Moses had waited all his life to enter. Instead he would die within sight of it.

Moses' failure at Meribah illustrates many of the shortcomings of the LIFE OVER GOD posture. First, rather than looking to a relationship with God, the LIFE OVER GOD view seeks to discern reliable principles. It reduces and limits God to a reproducible formula. It assumes that the way God has worked in the past is how he will continue to function indefinitely into the future and that once we have discovered these principles that govern God's actions, we may employ them with guaranteed outcomes. "God always—"; "God never—"; "God only—" are phrases used with flippant regularity in Christian communities, and they usually indicate the LIFE OVER GOD posture is present. With absolute certainty that we have figured out how God operates, or at least how he's ordained the world to operate, we place our trust in "God's principles" rather than in God himself. This is a serious error, as Moses tragically discovered.

The formulaic approach to the Christian life is perhaps most evident among church leaders—those responsible, like Moses, with leading God's people and providing for their spiritual nourishment. Ministry conferences and resources are saturated with promises of guaranteed outcomes and proven effectiveness. A children's ministry event in 2009 was promoted with rhetoric such as, "Dream dreams. Imagine possibilities. And get the tools you need to make them happen . . . You'll walk away with a customized plan to give your ministry guaranteed success."[14]

The message and tone of this ad are commonplace in marketing materials targeting pastors. Perhaps the most overused word in ministry circles—particularly those in more affluent communities—is *effective*. Everyone is eager to find the most effective principles for church growth, discipleship, worship, and outreach. The quest for effectiveness drives pastors to attend seminars and purchase books.[15]

Effectiveness is an odd value to be held in such high esteem by those of us who claim belief in a sovereign and unsearchable God. To guarantee effectiveness requires one to be in control over every variable and aspect. But if we are in control of the outcomes, where does that leave God? A friend once asked me, "If God's Spirit left your church, would anyone notice?" Put another way, if everything happening can be explained by human causality, then why do we need God?

Our insatiable need for control is what makes LIFE OVER GOD so attractive. And this need for control is inexorably linked to fear. Moses was frightened of the angry Israelites, so he took control of the situation by trusting in his proven staff. Church leaders may fear their congregations, their denominational leaders, or they may simply fear their own insignificance. So they consume any resources guaranteeing them an effective outcome. And we have plenty to fear in a world where families are dissolving at an alarming rate and the economy is volatile, so we look for divine principles to help us navigate through the turbulence.

But the sense of control and autonomy offered by the LIFE OVER GOD posture comes with a heavy price. By marginalizing God's place, or eliminating him altogether, LIFE OVER GOD leaves us in control. God's part was finished when he gave us the principles—the watchmaker has given us the owner's manual for life, and now we are responsible for following the instructions. Implementing God's principles and the outcomes are left on our shoulders. But this also means we have no one to blame when outcomes are not as expected. Unlike Buffalo Bills wide receiver Steve Johnson, we cannot send an angry tweet to God when we drop a pass in the end zone. As Uncle Ben said to a young Peter Parker (a.k.a. Spiderman), "With great power comes great responsibility."

This is the second terrible shortcoming of LIFE OVER GOD—it does not take away the burden of fear we carry. While promising to alleviate fears by giving us control of our lives through proven (even divine) formulas, it actually saddles us with a degree of responsibility we were never intended to carry. The need to manage every variable, control every minutia, and ensure we are following the prescribed principles makes fear even more potent.

Again, we see this vividly among church leaders. A study found that clergy in the United States are leaving the ministry at a rate of fifteen hundred per month.[16] Counselors studying the trend found that many pastors could no longer withstand the desperate need to validate their pastoral leadership by growing their church's attendance. The belief that a church's numerical growth or decline is the direct result of one person's leadership is only possible with a LIFE OVER GOD perspective. There is no room for mystery or the unsearchable movements of God. Church growth is a matter of implementing the right formulas. A minister whose church does not grow, therefore, is simply an ineffective leader using the wrong principles. For the fifteen hundred who throw in the towel every month, LIFE OVER GOD did nothing to remove their fears or alleviate their burdens.

But what about those who are successful? What about the people who implement God's principles for life, business, or ministry and find the outcomes to be wonderful? Surely their experience proves that principles can be the guiding force of the Christian life. This is the third great failure of the LIFE OVER GOD approach—it causes us to gauge success based on effective outcomes rather than faithfulness to God's calling. While studies may be able to tell us which principles of life, business, and ministry *work*, a research method has not yet been created that can determine whether a principle is *right*. In many places we simply assume that God values effectiveness as much as we do. We conclude, therefore, that the most effective principle is automatically the one God would have us employ. Once again we remove the need for prayer, spiritual discernment, or God's active participation in the process in favor of a utilitarian ethic.

Earlier I skipped a crucial part of the story of Moses at Meribah. He disobeyed God by striking the rock with the staff rather than speaking to it, and he was held responsible for his irreverence. But was Moses effective? Yes! We are told that after striking the rock twice, "water came out abundantly."[17] It seems that God performed a miracle *in spite of* Moses and not *because of* him. From any human perspective Moses was a success. His ministry was immensely effective. Had he lived in our time, Moses would be writing books and teaching seminars on "3 Effective Principles for Drawing Water from Rocks." But while everyone else praised Moses, the Lord remained unimpressed.

LIFE OVER GOD exchanges a relationship with him for applicable principles. It fails to alleviate our fears by stating that we are ultimately responsible for every outcome in our lives. And finally, even when things go as planned, it may leave us far outside the boundaries of what God intended.

Ultimately atheism, deism, and even living by "Christian" principles cannot deliver us from the cycles of fear and control that plague humanity. The dream is appealing—a world of peace and unity, a world without fear, and a world where proven formulas provide a sense of security. But it's a dream that cannot be fulfilled because the LIFE OVER GOD posture repeats and perpetuates the rebellion of humanity in Eden. In it we seek to take God's place by denying his existence or by marginalizing him as an optional or irrelevant factor. As a result, LIFE OVER GOD can only end in one place—a life *without* God. And that means no life at all.

4

Life *From* God

The Inkblot

Every semester Scot McKnight, professor of religious studies at North Park College in Chicago, gives his students a test on the first day of his Jesus class. The test begins with a series of questions about what the students think Jesus is like. Is he moody? Does he get nervous? Is he the life of the party or an introvert? The twenty-four questions are then followed by a second set—with slightly altered language—in which the students answer questions about their own personalities.[1]

McKnight is not the only one who has administered this exam; it has been field tested by other professionals as well. But the results are remarkably consistent—everyone thinks Jesus is just like them. McKnight added, "The test results also suggest that, even though we like to think we are becoming more like Jesus, the reverse is probably more the case: *we try to make Jesus like ourselves.*"[2] McKnight's personality questionnaire confirms what the French philosopher Voltaire said three centuries ago:

"If God has made us in his image, we have returned him the favor."[3]

The Jesus personality test functions much like the inkblot test devised by Hermann Rorschach for use in psychotherapy. A therapist shows a patient an inkblot and asks, "What do you see?" The blot does not resemble anything, so whatever the patient "sees" is really a projection of what is in his own mind. If the patient says "a flower," the therapist may conclude the subject is normal. But if he answers "a skull with blood dripping from the eye sockets"—well, that's why the men in white coats are on speed dial.

Once we understand our human tendency to give God a makeover in our own image, then asking a person "What is God like?" can be a kind of religious Rorschach test because we tend to project our own identities onto God. We assign him our personalities, our values, and our biases. We have seen this in the two postures already explored. LIFE UNDER GOD views him as a capricious deity who must be appeased in order to garner blessings and avoid punishment. God's volatility suited the fears of the ancient world in which superstition ruled life and culture. The LIFE OVER GOD posture imagines him to be the opposite—a rational and predictable calculation, a watchmaker whose laws and principles govern the world in his place. This God clearly reflects the post-Enlightenment age that gave rise to secularism, deism, and atheism.

But the contemporary Western world is not primarily driven by ancient superstition or natural science. We live in an age driven by the economics of conspicuous consumption. To paraphrase Madonna, we live in a material world, and we are material girls. So when we look at the God inkblot, most contemporary people project their own consumer values and identities onto the divine.

Christian Smith, a sociologist from the University of North Carolina, spent years studying the religious lives of teenagers. He concluded that most view God as a "combination divine butler and cosmic therapist."[4] God exists to help them through their problems and achieve what they desire. Smith said that those holding this view of God are "primarily concerned with one's own happiness in contrast to focusing on glorifying God, learning obedience, or serving others."[5] When asked why most teens view God as a butler or therapist, Smith concluded it was because most of their parents hold the same understanding of God.

Smith's research verifies what McKnight and others have consistently found—people make God in their own image. Smith's broader sampling of Americans found that what most of us hold in common is a consumer worldview, therefore we believe in a God who exists to satisfy our consumer desires. When contemporary and relatively affluent people look at the God inkblot, they don't necessarily see the God revealed in the Bible or even the God presented by rational science or superstitious traditions. They see a divine butler, a cosmic therapist, a holy vending machine who dispenses the wares and wisdom they desire.

This is the essence of the LIFE FROM GOD posture—God exists to supply what we need or desire. And although my tone may already be dismissive, there is some merit to this view of God. Scripture reminds us repeatedly that all we have comes *from* God. Everything that lives draws its life from God,[6] and he is the "Father of lights" from whom comes "every good gift and every perfect gift."[7] And Jesus calls us to ask God for what we need.[8] But the LIFE FROM GOD posture has a tendency to overemphasize this single aspect of the divine-human relationship. It makes receiving God's gifts the entirety of our religious lives, and this is where the posture begins to break down.

Consider LIFE FROM GOD in its most extreme form—the prosperity gospel (also known as the health-and-wealth gospel or the name-it-and-claim-it gospel). Quoted in *Time* magazine's article titled "Does God Want You to Be Rich?" television preacher Joyce Meyer said, "Who would want to get in on something where you're miserable, poor, broke and ugly and you just have to muddle through until you get to heaven? I believe God wants to give us nice things."[9] Perhaps Meyer believes this because she wants to have nice things. She was actually investigated by the United States Senate because of her opulent lifestyle.[10] Inkblot, anyone?

The LIFE FROM GOD posture is so appealing because it

doesn't ask us to change. What we desire, what we seek, what we do, and how we live—all shaped by consumerism—are not disrupted. Our values and way of life are simply projected onto God and incorporated into a religious system in which we receive divine assistance to meet our desires. In this way LIFE FROM GOD is nothing more than consumerism with a Jesus sticker slapped on the bumper.

The Orbit

LIFE FROM GOD is fueled by our consumer culture, but people have not always been defined by consumption. Consumers— like the goods they buy—were made, not born. The advent of mass production during the Industrial Revolution created previously unimaginable quantities of goods—far more than the market needed. Manufacturers suddenly required a way to artificially increase demand for their products to keep the economy steaming along. Advertising was born.

Ads became the prophets of capitalism—turning the hearts of the people toward the goods they didn't know they needed. Ads subtly or overtly promised comfort, status, success, happiness, and even sex to people who purchased their wares. Today, according to the *New York Times*, each person is exposed to thirty-five hundred desire-inducing advertisements every day. Rodney Clapp wrote, "The consumer is schooled in insatiability. He or she is never to be satisfied—at least not for long. The consumer is tutored that people basically consist of unmet needs that can be appeased by commodified goods and experiences."[11]

More than a century of marinating in this stew of products,

ads, and desire has transformed the way people see themselves and the world. Although lack of self-control has always plagued humanity, for the first time in history, an economic system has been created that relies on it. If people began suppressing their desires and consuming only what they needed, our economy would collapse. To prevent this, satisfying personal desires has become sacrosanct.

Following the attacks of September 11, 2001, Americans were told that refraining from buying, traveling, or continuing our materialistic lifestyle would be "letting the terrorists win." The message stood in contrast with the one given after the last major attack on American soil—the attack on Pearl Harbor in 1941. During World War II, President Roosevelt asked citizens to ration many goods needed for the war effort. During that conflict, sacrifice—not consumption—was honored as a core American value. How times have changed.

Now amid the global economic recession that began in 2008, economists point to runaway debt and overspending as the cause of the collapse. But government leaders did not call citizens to cut their spending or pay down their credit card debt. Instead they tried to "jump-start" the economy by issuing stimulus checks and telling Americans to spend their way out of the recession. All this reveals that consumerism is more than an economic system—it is a belief system. Consumption has come to define our lives, our government, and even our spirituality.

SELF

In 1955 an economist said, "Our enormously productive economy demands that we make consumption our way of life, that we convert the buying and use of goods into rituals, that we seek our spiritual satisfaction, and our ego satisfaction, in consumption."[12] And that is exactly what has occurred.

In the last chapter we looked at Newton's apple and how the Enlightenment understood the cosmos. LIFE OVER GOD says that at the core of the universe stands a set of immutable natural laws or principles. The more ancient LIFE UNDER GOD posture believes the gods' capricious will is at the core. What does the LIFE FROM GOD posture place at the core of the universe? Rooted in the values of consumerism and its focus on the fulfillment of personal desires, LIFE FROM GOD believes that if you peel away the layers of the cosmos, at its center you will find—yourself!

Consumerism is a supremely narcissistic worldview in which everything's value is determined by its usefulness to me. I stand at the center while everything and everyone orbits around me. This gives rise to utilitarian ethics.

Consider the way we shop. Little, if any, thought is given to the story behind a product, the people who made it, or the lives it affects. We act as if the item appeared magically on the shelf simply for our use, and when it is no longer useful we are justified in throwing it away and buying a new one. This same utilitarian mind-set can be applied to people. When a marriage is no longer satisfying my desires I can end it and try a new one. When a church community is no longer meeting my needs, I will attend a different one. And the fact that there are more men, women, and children in slavery today than at any other time in history—approximately twenty-seven million—shows the tragic impact of this self-centered mind-set on the most vulnerable.[13] Horrors like slavery, sex-trafficking, abortion, euthanasia, and genocide are only possible when people are seen as commodities—measured by their usefulness and not by their inherent worth.

In the LIFE FROM GOD posture, God also carries no inherent value. Like everything else in the consumer worldview, God's value is determined by his usefulness. He orbits around us. "What have you done for me lately?" could be the mantra of the LIFE FROM GOD posture. Religion is a means to an end—a more spiritual method of achieving our desires whether they are the products of advertising or of nobler sources. Those who relate to God primarily as the Almighty Provider hold a decidedly one-dimensional understanding of him: God gives and we receive. But this does not mean everything we seek from God is selfish.

In the opening chapter I shared the story of the mother seeking God's help for her drug-addicted son. No one would equate her desire with the televangelist asking God for "nice things." But when we put aside the specific content of the request, we discover that both the distraught mother and the greedy preacher view God as an instrument—as a means to an end. They seek to use him to achieve their desires. What differentiates them is the object of their desire, not how they relate to God. It is certainly not wrong to ask God for things—he invites us to ask. But when this becomes the entirety of how we relate to him, we are placing ourselves at the center and expecting God to orbit around us. We are insisting that the Creator submit to the creature. We are seeking to control God in order to achieve our objectives. We are, once again, repeating the rebellion of Eden.

The Leper

With the self and its desires at the center, LIFE FROM GOD perpetuates our sinful instinct to control the divine and force him to do our bidding. But how well does LIFE FROM GOD do with the other dilemma of the human condition—fear?

As we have seen in previous chapters, fear is central to the human experience in this world, and every religious system is an attempt to deliver us from it. But consumerism, and the LIFE FROM GOD posture derived from it, takes a slightly different tack. Rather than removing our fears and pains, consumerism tries to distract us from them. Commodified goods and experiences are used to keep us amused—anesthetizing us from the unpleasant realities of our existence. Neil Postman explored this phenomenon at length in his influential book, *Amusing Ourselves to Death*. Amusement, he reminds us, literally means "to not think,"[14] in other words, to be distracted. Filling our lives with trivial possessions and experiences is an attempt to distract us from the fears and pains of life. "Let us eat and drink, for tomorrow we die."[15]

When we absorb this cultural value into our faith, God can be reduced to an instrument of amusement. He, or his church, supplies us with the means of distracting ourselves from our pains and fears. We seek worship experiences every week to soothe the struggles we are having at work or home. We stay busy involved with programming or events at the church. And we pray for God's material blessings that will make our lives more enjoyable or comfortable. Rather than helping us experience the joys, sorrows, victories, and defeats of life more acutely and from a higher point of view, a great deal of contemporary religion is designed to help us just get along, to make us more comfortable on the journey, and perhaps to keep us entertained with music and merchandise designed to be "safe for the whole family."

But distraction is not the same as deliverance. Consumerism and LIFE FROM GOD may numb our fears and pains, but it does not remove them. And ultimately LIFE FROM GOD offers us no redemptive explanation for the existence of pain and suffering in the world. C. S. Lewis reminded us that "God whispers to us in our pleasures, speaks to us in our conscience, but shouts to us in our pains: It is his megaphone to rouse a deaf world."[16]

Although fear and pain were not originally part of God's creation, he nonetheless uses them to call us back to himself. These unpleasant realities of our world make us long for something better; they make us search for a beauty behind the shadows. But when the center of life is fulfilling desires and avoiding pain, as the LIFE FROM GOD posture promotes, no redemptive purpose for pain can be given. It is merely something to be avoided and soothed. God may be shouting with his megaphone through our pain, but consumerism would have us put on our headphones and crank up the volume on our iPods. Comfort rather than deliverance becomes our ultimate goal.

Dr. Paul Brand was a physician who spent much of his life working with lepers in India. He discovered the real danger was that leprosy destroys the nerve endings in the body and lepers lose their ability to feel. While the inability to feel pain might sound like a blessing, it is ultimately a lethal curse. Without pain lepers are unaware when they have been injured. As a result, even a tiny wound or splinter can be left untreated and become infected, leading to the loss of limbs or even death.

After documenting this phenomenon and treating its effects, Dr. Brand said, "I thank God for pain, I cannot think of a greater gift I could give to my leprosy patients." When taken too far, the pursuit of comfort and the avoidance of pain can make us into spiritual lepers—we become incapable of experiencing the aches God uses to awaken us to the reality of sin and evil in the world and in ourselves. Dr. Brand continued, "Most people view pain as an enemy . . . yet, without it, heart attacks, strokes, ruptured appendixes, and stomach ulcers would all occur without any warning. Who would ever visit a doctor apart from pain's warnings?"[17]

Although no one enjoys feeling pain or fear, they play a vital role in our existence. Physically they help us stay alive in our dangerous world, and spiritually they awaken our souls to seek a beauty, a justice, and a freedom beyond what this present world can provide. By focusing on insulating ourselves from these unpleasant experiences and pandering to our consumer desires, LIFE FROM GOD cuts off the redemptive purpose of pain and fear. In our comfort we forget the One who alone can deliver us from our true ailment. Instead we seek lesser things.

This is certainly not a new temptation. Long before the propagation of consumer capitalism, God warned his ancient people about the dangers of comfort. While slaves in Egypt the people cried out to God for deliverance. They sought after him, and he heard their cries. But after rescuing his people, it becomes apparent that their hearts were set more on God's gifts than on God himself. As he led them to freedom in a good and fruitful land, the Lord repeatedly cautioned them not to forget him once they were comfortable.

> Take care lest you forget the LORD your God by not keeping his commandments and his rules and his statutes, which I command you today, lest, when you have eaten and are full and have built good houses and live in them, and when your herds and flocks multiply and your silver and gold is multiplied and all that you have is multiplied, then your heart be lifted up, and you forget the LORD your God, who brought you out of the land of Egypt, out of the house of slavery.[18]

But God's prediction proved to be accurate. Again and again Israel turned away from God in times of prosperity and peace. They became enamored with his good gifts, and these comforts distracted the people from seeking God himself. As their connection to God was reduced to one of seeking material blessing, they became spiritual lepers—unable to feel the pains and fears of life that had led their ancestors to seek God while slaves in Egypt. Seeing their greed and insincerity, the Lord declared through the prophet Isaiah, "This people draw near with their mouth and honor me with their lips, while their hearts are far from me."[19]

The Jerk

It sounds like the storyline from a soap opera: The youngest son of a millionaire determines that his father's estate is cramping his style. He decides to leave home to live a free and wild life in Las Vegas, or the French Riviera, or maybe the swinging resorts of Southeast Asia. But with no marketable skills, the arrogant young man wants to bankroll his independent life with his father's fortune. So before jetting off, the son empties the trust fund his father had established for him, tells his dad to drop dead, and walks out the door.

If this storyline were unfolding on our televisions, we would all mutter the same thing, "What a jerk."

Jesus told a very similar story at a dinner party two millennia ago. The parable of the prodigal son is recorded in Luke 15, and in the story Jesus told of a son who demanded his inheritance *before* his father's death—a request so disrespectful it was a capital crime.[20] But the father allowed the young man to take his half of the family fortune before leaving home for a distant country where "he squandered his property in reckless living."[21] (At this point in the story I imagine those listening to Jesus around the dinner table all muttered, "What a jerk." Some sentiments are universal and timeless.)

Jesus used the story of the prodigal son to illustrate God's relationship with his people. The parable shows God's character through the father and our rebellion through the son. The story is a vivid illustration of the LIFE FROM GOD posture—the son valued his father's gifts more than he valued his father. Ultimately the son only wanted what his benevolent and wealthy father could give him, and once he possessed it, the relationship was no longer necessary. He walked away.

LIFE FROM GOD is no different. By placing all our focus on receiving God's blessings and gifts, we behave just like the arrogant young man in the story—we value what God can do for us but not God himself. We seek a relationship with God as a utilitarian means to an end. And although we may praise him with our words, our hearts are set on what we hope to get from him. We become jerks cloaked in religiosity.

Perhaps the label *jerk* is too prosaic. We can easily exchange it for a more religious word—*idolater*. According to the Bible, an idolater is anyone who exalts a created thing to the place reserved for the Creator alone. We are called to love the Lord our God with all our hearts, but when some lesser things take possession of our hearts, we have fallen into idolatry. And I must note that these lesser things are rarely altogether bad. Tim Keller, in his book *Counterfeit Gods*, defined idols as "good things [turned] into ultimate things."[22] God has blessed us with many wonderful things in this world, but when these—rather than him—become the focus of our desire, we have fallen into the LIFE FROM GOD posture.

Jesus confronted this tendency numerous times with shocking tenacity. For example, he taught that "whoever loves father or mother more than me is not worthy of me, and whoever loves son or daughter more than me is not worthy of me."[23] This incredible statement strikes right at our inclination to make a good thing, such as family, into an ultimate thing. Elsewhere Jesus warned about the dangers of seeking wealth,[24] a comfortable home,[25] or a stellar reputation.[26] None of these things are bad; in fact each is very good. But Jesus knows how easily we can twist one of God's good gifts into an ultimate desire. It can take a place he alone is worthy to hold in our lives.

And yet so much of contemporary religion is focused on God's gifts rather than on God. We use God as a means of building or repairing our families; we use him as a sex therapist; he is our political advisor and our financial planner. From God's hand we seek family, sex, power, and wealth—but do we actually want God himself? We shouldn't be surprised to find that when we fixate on what we can attain *from* God, we fail to experience the peace of his presence in our lives.

Jean Twenge and her colleagues in the psychology department at San Diego State University analyzed mental health records collected between 1938 and 2007 from more than sixty-three thousand young adults. What they uncovered was a dramatic upturn in psychological problems since the 1930s— most notably depression. *ABC News* reported: "The researchers found that students today feel much more isolated, misunderstood and emotionally sensitive or unstable than in previous decades . . . In addition, teens today are more likely to be narcissistic, have poor self-control and to say they're worried, sad, and dissatisfied with life."[27]

Twenge and her team concluded that consumerism is a major reason for the rise in mental illness. "We have become a culture that focuses on material things," she said, "and less on relationships."[28]

A parallel phenomenon has happened in religious communities as we focus less energy on fostering a genuine relationship with God and more energy on acquiring his blessings. This may help explain why we have more religious resources, books, radio and television stations, ministries, and schools than ever before, and yet more people are leaving the church.[29] Maybe they've discovered what they really wanted from God can be achieved just as easily without him. Or perhaps they've gotten what they can from him and have left home for a metaphorical distant country.

The bankruptcy of the LIFE FROM GOD posture is also evident in the story Jesus told his dinner companions. Eventually the self-obsessed son became penniless and took a job feeding pigs. He went from comped martinis at the high-rollers table at the Belligio, to cleaning buffet trays at the Nickel Slot Emporium. In this broken state, the son developed a new plan. He would return home, apologize to his father, and realizing he had forfeited any rights he once possessed as an heir, he would ask his father for a job as a servant.[30] But had the jerk really changed? Had he really learned to value his father, or was he once again hoping to use his father to improve his circumstances? Does he want his father—or just a chance for employment away from the pigs?

Whether devotion or desperation motivated the son, it ultimately did not matter. Jesus said that when the father saw his son still a long way off, "he ran and embraced him."[31] The joy of having his son back overshadowed everything else. And before his son finished his apology or finished asking for a job, the father already had ordered a feast prepared to celebrate his son's return.[32]

When we look at God, we may see a reflection of our consumer selves—a divine vending machine to dispense our desires. But when God looks at us, he sees his child, created in his image, who is wholly and dearly loved.

5

Life *For* God

The H.O.D.

Students call it "the H.O.D."—the House of Despair. To pedestrians and motorists passing by, the H.O.D. looks like most other homes on the tree-lined suburban street. But inside, college students struggling with life and faith are numbing their pain with alcohol, drugs, sex, and raw conversations—all of which are prohibited by their Christian college, with the exception of raw conversation (which, ironically, may be the most difficult for students to find).

I first learned about the House of Despair years ago while mentoring two undergrads. In our one-on-one meetings each of these young men opened up about his struggles. To my ears their issues did not seem particularly extraordinary for their age. But each expressed a sense of isolation, as if he were the only one on campus carrying secret doubts. To varying degrees they each questioned the faith of their parents and community, they questioned God's role in their lives, they

questioned the college's policies, and they were especially consumed with what to do after graduation. They feared living
lives of insignificance.

"Who else do you talk to about these things?" I asked. "I
know a number of faculty members. They're good people who
would listen."

"Yeah, but it's just awkward," one student said. "Profs are
busy and it's kinda hard to open up to them in a fifteen-minute
office appointment."

"Have you tried the college counseling center?" I asked.

"It's completely booked all the time," he said. "It's the
only place students can go and talk confidentially on campus.
There's so much demand that a lot of us can't get in."

"What about just talking with other students on your floor?
I know you're not the only one with these kinds of questions."

"No way. You didn't go to a Christian school. You don't
understand the vibe on campus." The student went on to
describe his fear. "Everyone here has life figured out. They've
got God figured out. And they're going to change the world
for Christ. At least that's what they say. And if you begin to
question things, if you show signs of doubting any of it, you're
shunned. So you've got to keep up the facade that everything's
okay—that you're not a mess inside."

I pushed back on the student's assessment. Not *everyone* at
your school has *everything* figured out. And *shunned* is probably
too strong a word. "They're probably afraid of your openness
because deep down they carry the same fears and doubts," I
said. While this student's perception is exaggerated, I've spoken
with others who feel the same way.

"It's hard to be in the middle," another student told me.

"You are either part of the mainstream student body that plays by the rules and has life figured out, or you are part of the underground. There's no room in between."

Members of the "underground" were defined by a single behavior—drinking. Consuming alcohol is prohibited for the undergraduate students I've worked with at different Christian colleges. The schools each have a code of ethics that students and faculty adhere to that is more comprehensive than codes at secular universities, but not nearly as draconian as the requirements at fundamentalist religious colleges.

"I don't drink because I like the alcohol," one female student told me. "In fact, I usually don't drink at all. I just hold the beer in my hand."

"Then why take the risk of being caught and disciplined?" I asked.

"Because drinking is how you know who's safe. When you drink with another student, you know that you can trust them. You've both broken the code of ethics—it's a sign that you can be honest about other things too. They're a safe person—you don't have to pretend with them."

After talking with a half-dozen "underground" students, I came to see that most were more complicated than the rebellious church-kid image they had been assigned. They were struggling with identity and faith and longing for a safe place to process their angst. That safe place became the House of Despair. At the H.O.D., drinking functioned as an alternative code of ethics—one that valued authenticity more than sobriety. And most of the students had not abandoned their faith in Christ; they were just looking for something more robust and real than institutional Christianity. Those who had given up on the search sometimes soothed their pain with more potent devices—usually drugs or sex.

After two years of journeying with these students, I decided they needed an alternative to the House of Despair—a safe place to talk and process without fear of judgment and where alcohol was not the price of admittance. I started meeting with groups more regularly for open conversation. Anyone was welcome, but I left it to students to invite others they thought could benefit from the groups.

The gatherings had only three rules: be honest, be gracious, and be present. That meant no phones and no phoniness. The students determined what we discussed. Topics ranged from the doctrine of hell to the pressure to find a spouse. I usually facilitated the conversation, asked questions, and tried to listen without judgment.

One night the students agreed that we should talk about habitual sin. "What do we do about sins we've struggled with for years and years?" one asked. "I've just given up trying to stop," said another. In private conversations I had discovered that some wrestled with Internet pornography and others with drugs. I learned that to these students anything sexual or chemical was seen as particularly sinful while little self-reflection went toward other vices like anger, greed, pride, or dishonesty.

"To get started let's go around and answer a question," I suggested. "I don't want to know what your particular sin is. Instead I want to know how you think God views you in the midst of your sin." The students became still. After a minute or two, the first one began to share.

"I think God is disappointed with me," he said. "I come from a great family with godly parents. I've been given everything imaginable, including a great education. And now I'm in college being prepared to impact the world for Christ. I think God's really disappointed when I sin because 'to whom much is given, much is expected.' God expects better from me."

"That's how I feel too," said another student. "How am I going to achieve what God wants from me if I'm still stuck in these same sins again and again?"

"My parents were students at a Christian college in the early '90s when a revival broke out," another student shared. "A bunch of grads that year became missionaries and pastors. They were on fire for God. And here I am consumed by sin day after day. I don't feel like I'm supposed to be here. I know I'm not who God wants me to be."

It took about an hour for everyone around the table to share. Some could only talk through their tears. In one form or another, every student gave the same answer—God is disappointed with me because of my ongoing struggles with some behavior. He expects more from me. And he cannot use me to accomplish his work in the world until I clean up my act.

"How many of you were raised in a Christian home?" I asked. They all raised their hands. "How many of you grew up in a Bible-centered church?" All the hands stayed up. "This is incredible!" I said, shaking my head in disbelief. "You've all spent eighteen or twenty years in the church. You've been taught the Bible from the time you could crawl, and you attend Christian colleges, but not one of you gave the right answer. Not one of you said that in the midst of your sin God still loves you."

I did not blame the students for this failure. Somewhere in their spiritual formation they were taught, either explicitly or implicitly, that what mattered was not God's love for them, but how much they could accomplish *for* him. That night I finally understood why they called it the House of Despair.

The Mission

In the last chapter we looked more closely at the LIFE FROM GOD posture and the way it complements the values of our consumer culture. It views God as a divine vending machine who exists to supply our needs and desires. Because consumerism has come to dominate our culture, we should not be surprised to find LIFE FROM GOD widely popular today. And the prevalence of this posture has been the source of endless consternation on the part of church leaders. I have heard church members focused on receiving blessings *from* God labeled "consumer Christians," "lazy Christians," and even "fat Christians." They are seen as spiritually lethargic and a drain on church resources. "They just take and take and take," one pastor told me, "and the moment you ask them to give something, they're gone."

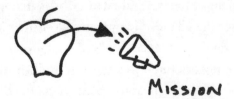

MISSION

The response to fat, lethargic Christians is usually a rigorous exercise routine. Ministries use many different devices to motivate people to serve, engage, and give; but their goal is the same—to transform their members from a posture of living *from* God to a posture of living *for* him. I've heard this goal articulated in a number of different ways. Some hope to move people "from taking to giving." Another church talks about "making spectators into participants." And I heard one church leader say his goal is "turning consumers into servants." Sometimes the LIFE FOR GOD posture is applied to whole congregations and not just individuals. Church leaders will often discuss the challenge of becoming an "outward-focused church" rather than an "inward-focused" one. The former being concerned with the world and the latter fixated on what color carpet to install in the church nursery.

The LIFE FOR GOD posture is especially evident within activist streams of Christianity. Evangelicalism is a prime example. Among more traditional evangelicals the emphasis has been on evangelism—the verbal proclamation of the gospel and persuasion of nonbelievers toward faith in Christ. Pastors and missionaries, those perceived as giving their full attention to this task, are particularly esteemed for devoting their lives to God's mission. Within these communities it is generally considered a victory when someone decides to leave their secular profession to enter "full-time Christian ministry." In the person's previous role, he or she may have volunteered a few hours each week at the church or given financially toward the mission, but now the person will be even more effective for God's kingdom—or so the logic goes.

Among younger evangelicals there is a push to broaden the scope of God's mission in the world. While not abandoning the importance of evangelism, some are eager to incorporate compassion and justice as central to the church's work. Debates rage about the validity of these pursuits and whether they are as urgent as rescuing souls, but the traditional and younger evangelicals agree that we are to live our lives *for* God by accomplishing his mission however we may define it.

Here we discover what lies at the center of the LIFE FOR GOD posture. If you recall, LIFE UNDER GOD believes divine will is at the center of the cosmic apple. LIFE OVER GOD says that natural law or principles are at the core. And LIFE FROM GOD places the self with its desires at the center. Cutting open the LIFE FOR GOD's cosmic apple would reveal a mission at the core. Some great goal—understood to be initiated by God and carried forward by us—defines everything and everyone. An individual is either *on* the mission, the *object* of the mission, an *obstacle* to the mission, an *aid* to the mission, or a fat Christian who *should* be on the mission.

The college students I met with had marinated in this "LIFE FOR GOD stew" all their lives. The people celebrated in their communities were those who had sacrificed and accomplished the most for Christ and his kingdom, and the message they heard repeatedly was the importance of transforming the world for God. They had come to view themselves entirely based on what they were able to accomplish on God's behalf. Even the presence or absence of sin in their lives was seen through this lens—how effective they could be *for* God.

Adding gravity to this posture are the innumerable biblical texts affirming and celebrating a life lived in service to God. No one illustrates this better than the apostle Paul. After a miraculous conversion, Paul was called by God to carry the message of Jesus throughout the Roman Empire and well beyond the Jewish community where the earliest Christians emerged.[1] This calling occupied the remainder of Paul's life as he tenaciously and faithfully took the gospel from city to city. He proclaimed the good news, taught converts, planted churches, and raised up leaders to take his place before moving on. And along the way he faced unimaginable difficulties including beatings, imprisonment, and shipwrecks.

Through it all Paul referred to himself as a "servant of Christ Jesus." When in prison, he called himself a "prisoner for Christ Jesus."[2] Paul strove to see others come to know Christ. He said, "I have become all things to all people, that by all means I might save some. I do it all for the sake of the gospel."[3] Paul was clearly a man on a mission, and the mission dominated his life.

The calling of Paul and the other apostles to carry the gospel forward permeates the New Testament. And while the mission of God is immensely important, as we will discuss in later chapters, many in the activist streams of the church see little else when they engage the Scriptures. As a result, they err by making mission the irreducible center of the Christian life. I don't wish to be misunderstood; I, too, long to see more Christians engage in the good work God has called us to, but a life spent *for* God is not what even Paul desired most for himself or others. Although God's mission dominated his life, it did not define it. A more careful reading of Paul's letters reveals something remarkable—everything in the apostle's life, including God's mission, took a backseat to his paramount goal: God himself.

While in prison, Paul wrote to the church in Philippi saying, "I count everything as loss because of the surpassing worth of knowing Christ Jesus my Lord. For his sake I have suffered the loss of all things and count them as rubbish, in order that I may gain Christ and be found in him."[4] Paul's language here is telling. When he wrote of "knowing" Christ, the word did not mean an intellectual knowledge *about* someone, but rather an intimate and *experiential* knowledge. This personal connection with Christ is what Paul valued above all else, and why he could find joy even while in chains.

And when Paul expressed his deepest desire for others, it was not that they would do more *for* God or transform the world for Christ and his kingdom, as good and important as such service may be. Instead he told believers to "make it your ambition to lead a quiet life: You should mind your own business."[5] Coming from Paul these are important words. After all, no one could rightly describe Paul's life as "quiet"—he caused havoc and even riots in the cities he visited. But he understood that his particular apostolic calling was not to be universally applied. And when he did articulate a universal goal for all Christians it was not strictly missional:

> I bow my knees before the Father . . . that according to the riches of his glory he may grant you to be strengthened with power through his Spirit in your inner being, so that Christ may dwell in your hearts through faith—that you, being rooted and grounded in love, may have the strength to comprehend with all the saints what is the breadth and length and height and depth, and to know the love of Christ that surpasses knowledge, that you may be filled with all the fullness of God.[6]

Again, none of this dismisses the incredible importance of God's mission in the world or our particular calling within it. But as we discussed in the last chapter, an idol is a good thing made into an ultimate thing, and the temptation within activist streams of Christianity is to put the good mission of God into the place God alone should occupy. The irony is that in our desire to draw people away from the selfishness of the LIFE FROM GOD posture, we may simply be replacing one idol with another. This is the first failure of LIFE FOR GOD—it puts God's mission ahead of God himself. Paul, the most celebrated missionary in history, did not make this mistake. He understood that his calling (to be a messenger to the Gentiles) was not the same as his treasure (to be united with Christ). His communion *with* Christ rooted and preceded his work *for* him.

The danger of confusing these two things is very real. At the end of his Sermon on the Mount, Jesus gave a haunting description of those who have accomplished a great deal for God but did not ultimately desire Christ himself. "On that day many will say to me, 'Lord, Lord, did we not prophesy in your name, and cast out demons in your name, and do many mighty works in your name?' And then will I declare to them, 'I never knew you; depart from me, you workers of lawlessness.'"[7]

The Impact

Making God's mission into an idol is a common and serious fault of the LIFE FOR GOD posture because it perpetuates the rebellion of Eden; it is a more subtle way of dethroning God and replacing him with something we can control. But the damage caused by the LIFE FOR GOD posture extends far beyond this original sin. As with the postures we have already explored, LIFE FOR GOD fails to alleviate our fears and manages to amplify one fear in particular.

The college students often worried about what awaited them after graduation. This is a reasonable concern for any young adult, but for many of them the worry extends far beyond finding a job with benefits. They fixate, and some obsess, about "making a difference in the world." They fear living lives of insignificance. They worry about not achieving the right things—or not enough of the right things. Behind all of this is the LIFE FOR GOD belief that their value is determined by what they achieve. I've learned that when a student asks me, "What should I do with my life?" what he or she really wants to know is, "How can I prove that I am valuable?"

LIFE FOR GOD takes our fear of insignificance and throws gasoline on it. The resulting fire may be presented to the world as a godly ambition, a holy desire to see God's mission advance—the kind of drive evident in the apostle Paul's life. But when these flames are fueled by fear, they reveal none of the peace, joy, or love displayed by Paul. The relentless drive to prove our worth can quickly become destructive.

Remember, God's original intent for us was a mission. He called humanity to rule over the earth, to fill and subdue it, and to extend his creative order and beauty far beyond the confines of the garden of Eden. This work was to be accomplished in perpetual communion *with* God, and it was to be motivated not by a fear of insignificance, but by the assurance of God's love for us. After the rebellion and the breaking of our union with God, humanity retained a sense of mission, a desire to achieve and subdue the earth. But when this work is pursued without God and not empowered by his presence and love, what was intended to be good and life giving becomes twisted and destructive. And rather than finding our value in God as his beloved children, instead we try to find our value in the mission we are chasing.

Sometimes the people who fear insignificance the most are driven to accomplish the greatest things. As a result, they are highly praised for their good works, which temporarily soothes their fear until the next goal can be achieved. But there is a dark side to this drivenness. Gordon MacDonald called it "missionalism." It is "the belief that the worth of one's life is determined by the achievement of a grand objective." He said,

> Missionalism starts slowly and gains a foothold in the leader's attitude. Before long the mission controls almost everything: time, relationships, health, spiritual depth, ethics, and convictions. In advanced stages, missionalism means doing whatever it takes to solve the problem. In its worst iteration, the end always justifies the means. The family goes; health is sacrificed; integrity is jeopardized; God-connection is limited.[8]

What I was witnessing in the lives of the college students were the early symptoms of missionalism. The virus was introduced to them in childhood and had been incubated by well-intentioned churches, ministries, schools, and the wider evangelical subculture. With graduation looming, the students were feeling the pressure. It was, after all, their first opportunity to prove their worth through achievement.

Phil Vischer, the creator of VeggieTales, a successful series of Christian home videos and films featuring computer-generated fruits and vegetables, was raised in a LIFE FOR GOD environment. His experience reveals how the fear of being insignificant is implanted into young people. He said the heroes his community celebrated were "the Rockefellers of the Christian world"—those who were enterprising, effective, and who made a huge impact for God. They launched massive ministries or transformed whole nations. This led Vischer to conclude that impact was everything. "God would never call us from greater impact to lesser impact!" he wrote. "How many kids did you invite to Sunday? How many souls have you won? How big is your church? How many people will be in heaven because of your efforts? Impact, man!"[9]

But after losing his company in 2003, Vischer began to question the validity of the LIFE FOR GOD values he had inherited and that had driven his early career.

> The more I dove into Scripture, the more I realized I had been deluded. I had grown up drinking a dangerous cock-tail—a mix of the gospel, the Protestant work ethic, and the American dream . . . The Savior I was following seemed, in hindsight, equal parts Jesus, Ben Franklin, and Henry Ford. My eternal value was rooted in what I could accomplish.[10]

A professional crisis made Vischer pause and reexamine his posture with God, but for others the nagging discontent of a life lived for God manifests much more slowly. Consider what one pastor in his late thirties wrote: "The church is growing, and there's excitement everywhere. But personally I feel less and less good about what I'm doing. I'm restless and tired. I ask myself how long I can keep this all up. Why is my touch with God so limited? Why am I feeling guilty about where my marriage is? When did this stop being fun?"[11]

This leader is not alone. We mentioned earlier the study that revealed approximately fifteen hundred pastors leave the ministry every month due to conflict, burnout, or moral failure.[12] Others have shown how ministry rooted in the LIFE FOR GOD posture actually contributes to addictive behaviors. When the accolades that give pastors a sense of significance cease or never come at all, some pastors begin to nurse secret pleasures on the side to numb their pain.

Dave Johnson is pastor of Church of the Open Door near Minneapolis, Minnesota. When he first came to the church in 1980, it was a small congregation; but after twelve years of hard work for God, the congregation had grown into a megachurch. Johnson recalled, "I was empty. I was ready to quit if I didn't collapse first. I remember getting a plaque from some organization for being one of the ten fastest-growing churches in the city. But inside we were a mess. My personal life was a mess."

At the time Johnson believed that having a healthy soul and a successful ministry were mutually exclusive. Serving God required sacrifice—including the sacrifice of one's family and health. But the disconnect between the measurable success of his work and the emptiness of his soul was more than he could bear. Johnson said he and a few other leaders from the church "took the plaque into the woods, put it on a tree, and shot it full of holes with a rifle. We hated what it stood for."[13]

When church leaders function from this understanding of the Christian life, they invariably transfer their burden and fears to those in the pews. If a pastor's sense of worth is linked to the impact of his or her ministry, guess what believers under that pastor's care are told is most important? And so a new generation of people who believe their value is linked to their accomplishments is birthed. If the cycle continues long enough, an institutional memory is created in which the value of achievement for God is no longer questioned.

Leaders may be burning out at a rate of fifteen hundred per month, young people may be riddled with anxiety, and divorce rates in the church may be rising and families falling apart, but no one seems to stop and ask whether this is really what God intended the Christian life to be. No one asks, at least not out loud, how Paul could be filled with joy in prison while not accomplishing anything tangibly for God. They don't ask because that might slow things down. Remember, the work must go on. *Impact, man!*

The Jerk (part 2)

While examining the LIFE FROM GOD posture, we looked at the parable of the prodigal son.[14] If you recall, the son did not value a relationship with his father but only valued his father's wealth. He took what his father gave him, left home, and wasted the gifts on fast living. Eventually he was penniless and desperate—reduced to feeding pigs in a distant country. But when the son returned home to seek his father's mercy and a job as a servant, he was astonished to find his father overjoyed—running to embrace him with open arms.

But that's only half the story. The father also had an older son who was very different from his swinging sibling. He was reliable, obedient, and lived to do his father's bidding. But when the older son heard that his wayward brother had returned, and that his father had welcomed him and was throwing a party, he became incensed. In fact, when he heard the music and dancing in the house, he refused to join the celebration. Instead he held his own pity party out in the field.

True to his character, when the father discovered that his eldest son was not home, the father went out to find him. The father begged his older son to come to the party. But the son was furious. "Look, these many years I have served you, and I never disobeyed your command, yet you never gave me a young goat, that I might celebrate with my friends. But when this son of yours came, who has devoured your property with prostitutes, you killed the fattened calf for him!"[15]

When first hearing this story, many people sympathize with the older son. His anger seems justifiable. Why should the disobedient son get a party while the good son gets nothing? The two sons clearly represent two postures we've examined. The greedy younger son illustrates the core characteristic of LIFE FROM GOD, while the loyal older son exemplifies LIFE FOR GOD. But Jesus did not extol the older son either. In fact, his purpose in telling the parable is to show how *both* sons were lost—how both ways of relating to God miss the point. To see this we need to examine the older son's words more carefully, because in them we discover something disturbing.

Notice where the older son rooted his significance: "All these years I have served you, and I never disobeyed your command." The older son lived *for* his father. And for his service he *expected* a reward. In this way he really was not that different from the younger son. Neither boy was particularly interested in a relationship with his father; instead both were focused on what they might get from him. The younger son simply took what he desired while the older son, being a more patient and self-disciplined person, worked for it. Their methods were like night and day, but both sons desired the same thing and in neither case was it the father. In other words, both sons sought to *use* their father. Both were jerks, one just happened to be of a more socially acceptable variety.

Jesus told this parable at a gathering with Pharisees and scribes—very devoted religious leaders, men who drew a great deal of significance from their service for God. Was Jesus trying to tell them that there is something wrong with serving God or faithful obedience? Of course not. The problem comes when we find our significance and worth in serving or obedience. Obedience gave the older son, as it did the Pharisees, a sense of self-righteousness—a smug arrogance that became bitterness, resentfulness, and anger toward those deemed less valuable.

Jesus was not diminishing the older son's obedience, just as he was not endorsing the younger son's immorality. He was showing that both the LIFE FROM GOD and the LIFE FOR GOD postures fail to capture what God truly desires for his people. Pouring our lives into a mission that we believe pleases God is not the center of the Christian life. It is not what is going to remove our fears or unbind our captivity to sin. In order to discover what God cares about most, we must look more closely at the father's response to the older son in Jesus' story: "Son, you are always with me, and all that is mine is yours. It was fitting to celebrate and be glad, for this your brother was dead, and is alive; he was lost, and is found."[16]

What brought the father joy was not the older son's service but simply his presence—having his son *with* him. This was what the father cared about most, not his property or which son received more. While the sons were fixated on their father's wealth, the father was fixated on his sons. This is what they failed to understand, and it is what LIFE FROM GOD and FOR GOD fail to grasp. God's gifts are a blessing and his work is important, but neither can nor should replace God as our focus.

Like the younger son we often build our identities around what we receive from God. Or like the older son we find our value in how we serve God. A great deal of effort is expended in faith communities trying to transform people from younger sons into older sons. But this is a fool's errand, because what mattered most to the father was neither the younger son's disobedience nor the older son's obedience, but having his sons *with* him. And so it is with our heavenly Father. Reversing the rebellion of Eden and restoring what was lost can only be accomplished when we learn that at the center of God's heart is having his children *with* him.

6

Life *With* God

The Eucatastrophe

"What does LIFE WITH GOD look like?" That's the question I hear most often when discussing the five postures. The other four postures are usually grasped rather quickly because of their familiarity. They correspond with forms of religion most of us have either experienced or been exposed to. But we have a far more difficult time visualizing what a LIFE WITH GOD looks like because it is sadly so rare.

In chapter 1 we learned about the ancient mausoleum of Galla Placidia in Ravenna, Italy. Visitors herded into the mausoleum must stand elbow-to-elbow. In the darkness the odors become more acute. The ancient tomb smells, well, like an ancient tomb. Together with the overly perfumed and often sweaty tourists, it creates an unpleasant olfactory experience. The visitors closest to the exit may tolerate the discomfort for a few minutes before escaping for fresh air and daylight.

This captures the experience many have had with the

church and Christianity. They come expectantly but leave disappointed. Or they may still identify themselves as Christians but actually settle for a posture toward God quite different from the one intended by Christ. Trying to speak with these people about the wonders and beauty of LIFE WITH GOD is exceedingly difficult because they simply have no reference point for it. They cannot begin to imagine what it looks like; it has remained hidden behind the shadows cast by this dark world. As Brother Lawrence, a seventeenth-century monk, said about his rich communion with God, "Those only can comprehend it who practice and experience it."[1]

But there is hope. We are not left in the darkness forever. In the Galla Placidia those who are patient will experience an unexpected delight. Coins dropped into a donation box trigger the spotlights. Suddenly, and for just a few seconds, heaven is revealed—the mosaic is suddenly unveiled for all to see. Christ the Good Shepherd sits enthroned in an emerald and sapphire paradise, the iridescent swirls of previously invisible stars burst forth, and the smelly tourists are transported to another realm.

Like the mosaic ceiling in Ravenna, LIFE WITH GOD is so far beyond our imagination that it must be revealed to us. We cannot begin to imagine the beauty that exists behind the shadows. A light beyond ourselves must be turned on so that we can begin to see. And this is precisely what occurred when God took on flesh and made his dwelling among us.

The advent of Jesus Christ is what sets Christianity apart from other religions. We affirm that Christ is indeed Immanuel, God *with* us, and that in him the fullness of God was pleased to dwell. He is the image of the invisible God. And with Jesus an entirely different way of relating to God is revealed to us. Rather than stumbling in the darkness between forms of religion that are each a variation of fear and control (LIFE UNDER, OVER, FROM, and FOR GOD), through Christ the lights are turned on and our attention is drawn to an entirely different vision—LIFE WITH GOD.

J. R. R. Tolkien, the author of *The Lord of the Rings*, often employed a storytelling device he called *eucatastrophe*. A catastrophe is an unexpected evil, but Tolkien added the Greek prefix *eu-* meaning "good" to express the unexpected appearing of goodness. He defined it as "the sudden happy turn in a story which pierces you with a joy that brings you to tears." It has this effect on us "because it is a sudden glimpse of Truth" in which we "feel a sudden relief as if a major limb out of joint had suddenly snapped back."[2] Repeatedly in his stories the eucatastrophe occurs just as all hope appears to be lost. It is the moment the eagles swoop in for the rescue, the riders of Rohan arrive at the battle, or Gandalf the White appears with the breaking of the day.

RELATIONSHIP

To use Tolkien's language, the coming of Jesus Christ was a eucatastrophe. He is the light that gives us a sudden glimpse of truth. Our humanly devised ways of relating to God that never seem to satisfy are revealed to be out of joint. But in Christ things suddenly snap into place, and the result is joy.

His coming also shines a light onto a truth about the cosmos previously hidden from our sight. If you recall, each of the four popular postures has a different way of seeing the universe. LIFE UNDER GOD sees the world as governed by the capricious will of God. LIFE OVER GOD places immutable natural laws at the center. LIFE FROM GOD assumes the world orbits around the self and its desires. And LIFE FOR GOD sees a divine mission at the core of all things.

But in the opening words of John's gospel, which speak of Jesus' divinity and incarnation, we are given a very different vision of the universe. "In the beginning was the Word, and the Word was with God, and the Word was God. He was in the beginning with God."[3] It is one of the enduring paradoxes of the Christian faith—Jesus (the Word) existed before all things, and he was both *with* God and *was* God. From this passage, and numerous others, comes the Christian doctrine of the Trinity: one God eternally existing in three persons—God the Father, God the Son, and God the Holy Spirit. While a fuller exploration of the Trinity is beyond the scope of this book,[4] a basic understanding of the doctrine is critical toward understanding the Christian view of the cosmos.

If we peeled back the physical and metaphysical layers of time and space and peered into the very core of the universe, we would not discover divine will, natural law, personal desire, or global mission. Instead we would find God existing in eternal *relationship* with himself. This changes our view both of the world and why God created it. I like how Kevin DeYoung explained it: "With a biblical understanding of the Trinity we can say that God did not create in order to be loved, but rather, created out of the overflow of the perfect love that had always

100

existed among Father, Son, and Holy Spirit who ever live in perfect and mutual relationship and delight."[5]

The LIFE WITH GOD posture is predicated on the view that relationship is at the core of the cosmos: God the Father *with* God the Son *with* God the Holy Spirit. And so we should not be surprised to discover that when God desired to restore his broken relationship with people, he sent his Son to dwell *with* us. His plan to restore his creation was not to send a list of rules and rituals to follow (LIFE UNDER GOD), nor was it the implementation of useful principles (LIFE OVER GOD). He did not send a genie to grant us our desires (LIFE FROM GOD), nor did he give us a task to accomplish (LIFE FOR GOD). Instead God himself came to be *with* us—to walk with us once again as he had done in Eden in the beginning. Jesus entered into our dark existence to share our broken world and to illuminate a different way forward. His coming was a sudden and glorious catastrophe of good.

In this chapter we will look at what Jesus revealed about relating to God and how it is fundamentally different from the other four postures we have already explored. Then in the final three chapters we will see how a LIFE WITH GOD positions us to know true faith, hope, and love in a way not possible from other postures.

The Treasure

To begin we must understand how the LIFE WITH GOD posture differs from the other four. LIFE UNDER, OVER, FROM, and FOR GOD each seeks to *use* God to achieve some other goal. God is seen as a means to an end. For example, LIFE FROM GOD uses him to supply our material desires. LIFE OVER GOD uses him as the source of principles or laws. LIFE UNDER GOD tries to manipulate God through obedience to secure blessings and avoid calamity. And LIFE FOR GOD uses him and his mission to gain a sense of direction and purpose.

But LIFE WITH GOD is different because its goal is not to *use* God, its goal *is* God. He ceases to be a device we employ or a commodity we consume. Instead God himself becomes the focus of our desire. But before we can really desire God, we must have a clear understanding of who he is and what he is like. The reason most people gravitate to one of the other four postures is because they've never received a clear vision of who God is, and so they settle for something less.

My six-year-old son has a serious sugar addiction. I came to this realization when as a toddler he spotted a blotch of powdered sugar on the floor near a funnel cake stand at a minor league baseball stadium. He dropped to his knees and proceeded to lick the concrete. (His mother needed resuscitation.) Despite his obvious passion for sucrose, if I asked Isaac, "Would you like to try some *crème brûlée?*" he would immediately decline. The words *crème brûlée* might conjure images of vegetables or some other unappetizing adult cuisine in his imagination. But I knew he would respond differently if I asked, "Would you like some vanilla pudding, covered in sugar, and cooked with a blowtorch?"

The idea of combining large quantities of sugar with the forbidden danger of open flames is too much for any boy to resist. Even more compelling than my description would be actually watching the dessert's preparation. I would have to bind him to his chair to keep him from leaping at it.

Words, ideas, and even images only make sense when we have a frame of reference for them. While our problem of relating to God is far more than semantics, it has been my experience that when most people hear or think about God, they have a less than complete, and sometimes entirely flawed, vision of who he is. As a result, they do not tend to desire him. At best they see him as a useful instrument for achieving something more desirous. But if their vision were enlarged and corrected, if they could see his unrivaled beauty, grasp his unconditional love, perceive his radiant glory, and experience his untainted goodness, then it would become obvious that he is much more than a deity to simply tolerate or a device to employ. In other words, God would cease to be *how we acquire* our treasure, and he would *become* our treasure.

This was the great deception of the serpent in Eden—with his cunning questions he clouded humanity's vision of God. He caused the man and woman to question God's goodness and love. And with their vision of God blocked by shadows and distorted by lies, they settled for something less.

Consider the story the apostle Mark told in chapter 5 of his gospel. A man possessed by an "unclean spirit" approached Jesus on the beach. He had been driven from his village because he could not be controlled. Chains and ropes could not contain him; he screamed uncontrollably and cut and tortured himself day and night. Having mercy on the man, Jesus healed him.

When word reached the village about what had happened, the people came to the shore to see for themselves. "And they came to Jesus and saw the demon-possessed man . . . clothed and in his right mind, and they were afraid . . . And they began to beg Jesus to depart from their region. As he was getting into the boat, the man who had been possessed with the demons begged him that he might be with him."[6]

The different responses to Jesus in this story are telling. The townspeople had seen Jesus' power and were frightened by him. *Someone with such power could do incalculable damage. He might take over our village, enslave our families, take our wealth. Who knows what such a powerful person might do to us.* So, they begged Jesus to leave. But the man whom Jesus had healed had experienced more than his power—he had also seen his goodness. The healed man had a very different vision of Jesus and therefore a different response. He wanted to be *with* Jesus.

The same pattern holds true today. Those with an incomplete or tainted vision of God either want to use him or dismiss him. But when a full, clear, and rapturous vision of God is presented, we will not settle for anything less than being with him. This complete vision of God and his character comes not from within us, but is gifted to us in Jesus who "is the image of the invisible God."[7] And he made this very point repeatedly when talking to those who would follow him. He often asked what they were willing to leave behind in order to be with him— their wealth, their other relationships, their professions? With these difficult and sometimes offensive questions, Jesus was determining whether they were truly interested in him or just in what he might do for them. Many, like the villagers who begged him to leave, still failed to recognize his worth.

And yet those who saw Jesus' true value crawled over one another to be closer to him. This was particularly the case among the marginalized and forgotten in the society—the tax collectors, prostitutes, and sinners who had been denied access to God by the other religious postures of the day. These undesirables swarmed Jesus wherever he went—prompting the indignation of the religious leaders who had a vested interest in promoting their own posture of relating to God that excluded the hoi polloi.

The value of the kingdom of heaven, which Jesus equated with his own presence, was spoken of in similar terms. Jesus said,

> The kingdom of heaven is like treasure hidden in a field, which a man found and covered up. Then in his joy he goes and sells all that he has and buys that field. Again, the kingdom of heaven is like a merchant in search of fine pearls, who, on finding one pearl of great value, went and sold all that he had and bought it.[8]

One of the diagnostic questions I ask people when determining what posture they are living from is, *What is your treasure? What is the goal and desire of your life? What would you give everything to possess?* You can imagine the range of answers I have heard. But occasionally a person's eyes will sharpen as if they are looking at something or someone past me. A subtle smile will appear. And they will answer, "Christ. He is my treasure." That person has found the irreducible foundation of a LIFE WITH GOD.

Sadly, this is what many churches and ministries fail to

understand. The primary purpose of our worship gatherings, preaching, and programs should be to present a ravishing vision of Jesus Christ. When people come to see who he is and what God is like, treasuring him becomes the natural outcome. But in many places the vision of Christ remains hidden behind shadows while lesser glories—often some variation on the culture's values or the church's mission—are given the spotlight. And then we scratch our heads in bewilderment when people leave the church disappointed and unsatisfied or fail to engage. "My congregation needs a swift kick in the tail to share their faith," one pastor told me. What his people probably need is a clear vision of who Christ really is—a vision I'm guessing the pastor needs as well.

The Reunion

LIFE WITH GOD means first treasuring him above all else, and we are inspired to treasure him when he is revealed to us in Jesus Christ. But this alone does not answer the question we have set out to explore: *What does life with God look like?* A vision of God that causes us to treasure him is not the same as living *with* him. There are two additional components necessary to complete the picture.

Consider a young man who recently acquired his driver's license. He wants to start his new motorized life with a vintage Ford Mustang. First, the young man must have a *vision* of such a life, one that leads him to treasure the Mustang. But treasuring the Mustang is quite different from living *with* the Mustang. Two other things must occur. He must also be *united* with the Mustang. This may happen by purchasing it, by receiving it as a gift, or by stealing it. But until he *has* it he cannot have a life *with* it. Finally, his envisioned life will not be fulfilled when the Mustang is in his driveway. He must do more than possess it; he must *experience* it. He must take it for a drive, cruise the streets, and engage the machine.

This admittedly crude analogy can apply to our LIFE WITH GOD. Once we come to treasure him and not merely use him, two questions remain: How do we *unite* with God, and how do we *experience* him? LIFE WITH GOD entails all three—treasuring, uniting, and experiencing.

The Bible doesn't speak of "possessing God" the way one possesses or acquires a piece of property. He is not a passive object, like a vintage Mustang, to be purchased and put on display. The writers of the New Testament talked about being "united with" or "reconciled to" God. They used relational language to emphasize the interpersonal nature of the human-divine connection. When the apostle Paul spoke of being reconciled to God (as in 2 Corinthians 5), his language hinted at the fact that at one time humanity had lived in unity with God but that this state of unity was lost. As such we need to be brought back together—reconciled. As much as we might treasure God and desire him, there is something preventing us from living with him. That something is sin.

Remember, at the beginning in Eden the man and woman rebelled against God to seek an autonomous existence without him. This rebellion, which has been repeated by each of us, is manifested in countless ways—including religious varieties that seek to use or manipulate God—LIFE UNDER, OVER, FROM, and FOR GOD. As the prophet Isaiah rightly said, "All we like sheep have gone astray; we have turned—every one—to his own way."[9] And the consequence for breaking our union with God, the impact of separating ourselves from the Creator of life, is death. The rebellion of sin, which leads to death, must be overcome if we are to be united again with God. But how?

Thankfully, Jesus came not merely to be a beautiful revelation of who God is so that we might treasure him, but he also came to reconcile us to God so that our desire (and his) might be fulfilled. When John the Baptist saw Jesus, he declared, "Behold, the Lamb of God, who takes away the sin of the world!"[10] And Jesus declared, "The Son of Man came . . . to give his life as a ransom for many."[11]

This is why the cross is so central to Christian faith. On the cross Jesus took the penalty for our sin on himself. He died our death. While nailed to a Roman cross he shouted, "My God, why have you forsaken me?" He endured a kind of separation from God that the rest of humanity deserved. The prophet Isaiah described sinful humanity as wandering sheep, but his prophecy continued to foresee Jesus' work of taking away our sin: "All we like sheep have gone astray; we have turned—every one—to his own way, and the LORD has laid on him the iniquity of us all."[12]

With the barrier of sin and death removed by Jesus on the cross, the way has been opened for us to be reconciled to God;

to be united with him once again. All that remains is to trust in what Christ has done. This is called faith. Faith in Jesus Christ is how we are united with God.

For those familiar with the Bible or who have had significant church experience, this may all sound very familiar. But in many presentations of the Christian message, uniting with God (being reconciled through the cross) is divorced from any notion of treasuring God. As a result, many end up expressing faith in Christ so their sins can be forgiven, but they do so either as a ticket to heaven or as a pass out of hell, *not* because they actually desire God. When this happens we fall back into the trap of *using* God. In this popular understanding of the gospel, God becomes a means, a device, rather than the end and the treasure. This is not the Christian gospel. John Piper captured the problem well:

> Christ did not die to forgive sinners who go on treasuring anything above seeing and savoring God. And people who would be happy in heaven if Christ were not there, will not be there. The gospel is not a way to get people to heaven; it is a way to get people to God. It's a way of overcoming every obstacle to everlasting joy in God. If we don't want God above all things, we have not been converted by the gospel.[13]

As we saw in chapter 1, from the beginning in Genesis straight through to the end of Revelation, God's focus and desire has been to be with his people. He walked in the garden with the man and the woman and sought to rule over creation *with* them. And the crescendo of history in Revelation celebrates the reunion of God and humanity: "Behold, the dwelling place of God is with man. He will dwell with them, and they will be his people, and God himself will be with them as their God."[14]

Fulfilling God's desire to be with us is why Jesus went to the cross. He did not die merely to inaugurate a mission (LIFE FOR GOD) or to give us a second chance at life (LIFE FROM GOD). He did not endure the horrors of the cross just to demonstrate a principle of love for others to emulate (LIFE OVER GOD) or to appease divine wrath (LIFE UNDER GOD). While each of these may be rooted in truth and affirmed by Scripture, it is only when we grasp God's unyielding desire to be *with* us that we begin to see the ultimate purpose of the cross. It is more than a vehicle to rescue us from death; it transports us into the arms of Life. The cross is how we acquire our treasure. It is how we find unity with God.

The Now

So far we have seen that a desire for a LIFE WITH GOD is kindled when we see him as he truly is and begin to treasure God and not merely use him. Second, LIFE WITH GOD is made possible because of what Jesus has done on the cross; he has removed the barrier of sin and death that separates us from God. We have been united with him through Christ.

Sadly this is where many people stop their exploration of Christian faith. Having trusted Christ and the sufficiency of his sacrifice on the cross, they assume any further experience of God must wait until death, when they will be set free and ushered into his presence. This view dismisses the remaining years of life as an inconvenient delay before entering eternity, and it sees the earth as little more than God's waiting room. But this is not at all consistent with what Scripture teaches.

The fact is, having been united with God through Christ, we are invited to experience LIFE WITH GOD *now*. It is true that we will experience him most fully when the world and we are completely set free from the malady and malice of sin, but that does not mean we cannot experience God in the present. The apostle Paul wrote about our capacity to know God today, however imperfectly, and to know him fully in the time to come: "For now we see only a reflection as in a mirror; then we shall see face to face. Now I know in part; then I shall know fully, even as I am fully known."[15]

But Paul and the other apostles also stressed the reality of knowing God in the present, of experiencing him today![16] And it is important to reiterate that in the Bible to "know" is not merely an intellectual or cognitive knowledge. The word refers to a personal, intimate relationship. It is possible to have an interpersonal, experiential, interactive relationship with God well before one's body assumes room temperature. I appreciate the way Dallas Willard expressed this wonderful truth:

> The treasure we have in heaven is also something very much available to us now. We can and should draw on it as needed, for it is nothing less than God himself and the wonderful society of his kingdom even now interwoven in my life. Even now we "have come to Mount Zion and to the city of the living God, the heavenly Jerusalem, and to countless angels, and to the assembled church of those born

earlier and now claimed in the heavens; and to God who discerns all, to the completed spirits of righteous people, and to Jesus the mediator of a new agreement" (Hebrews 12:22–24). This is not by-and-by, but now. What is most valuable for any human being, without regard to an after-life, is to be a part of this marvelous reality, God's kingdom now. Eternity is now ongoing. I am now leading a life that will last forever.[17]

Returning to our vintage Mustang analogy, in Christ we not only have been united with our treasure, we also have been handed the keys and invited to take a drive. But sadly some people have never been taught how. The notion of having a "personal relationship with God" is familiar, even cliché, in some Christian traditions. But for many of the younger men and women I have counseled, a relationship with God means little more than reading the Bible for fifteen minutes a day, asking him for help with your struggles, and attending church with some regularity. They have no greater vision.

As with the previous two steps in the LIFE WITH GOD posture (treasuring and uniting), Jesus also modeled what experiencing God looks like. The gospel writers recorded that Jesus frequently sought solitude for prayer. He wanted time alone with his Father. And his disciples, those closest to him, were intrigued by his practice. He did not pray like other rabbis of his day. So they asked him, "Lord, teach us to pray."[18] The prayer Jesus taught them has been embraced by Christians throughout history. The Lord's Prayer[19] is far more than a list of requests offered up to God; it is the pattern of a life in communion *with* him.

For many people prayer is seen primarily as a form of *communication*—the way we talk to God. In some traditions it is believed that God may even speak to us in prayer. But in both cases prayer has a definition limited to communication. And while that is certainly part of prayer, it does not capture the entirety of what Jesus or his apostles said about it. Jesus did not experience his Father's presence merely in his times of solitude or while speaking to him, but also during his hours healing, teaching, and serving others. He spoke of his utter dependence on his Father: "The Son can do nothing of his own accord, but only what he sees the Father doing. For whatever the Father does, that the Son does likewise."[20] And Jesus repeatedly spoke of dwelling with the Father in present unity: "The words that I say to you I do not speak on my own authority, but the Father who dwells in me does his works. Believe me that I am in the Father and the Father is in me."[21]

While Jesus certainly prayed vocally both in private and public, these utterances did not encompass the fullness of his relationship with his Father. A fuller reading of the Gospels shows that Jesus lived in constant *communion* with the Father even when no words were used. This fuller understanding of prayer is often perplexing to those who have only known prayer as communication.

For example, in the 1980s Dan Rather interviewed Mother Teresa. The CBS anchor asked her, "When you pray, what do you say to God?"

"I don't say anything," she replied. "I listen."

"Okay," Rather said, taking another shot at it. "When God speaks to you, then, what does he say?"

"He doesn't say anything. He listens."

Rather didn't know how to continue. He was baffled.

"And if you don't understand that," Mother Teresa added, "I can't explain it to you."[22]

This communion view of prayer is what Paul meant when he commanded Christians to "pray without ceasing."[23] Paul was calling us to live as Jesus did—in constant connection with God even when no words are exchanged. This is made possible by the presence of God's Spirit within us.

Jesus promised to send the Holy Spirit to his people (John 14). "In that day you will know that I am in my Father, and you in me, and I in you."[24] In the same discourse he invited us to "abide in me, and I in you. As the branch cannot bear fruit by itself, unless it abides in the vine, neither can you, unless you abide in me. I am the vine; you are the branches."[25] This call to dwell or abide is an ongoing state of being, not an invitation to chat once in a while. We are invited to live in ongoing communion with God, and this is made possible through the presence of his Spirit who is with us.

By granting us his presence through the Holy Spirit, we can, as Dallas Willard said, have our treasure now. We can live in constant, unending communion with God. Thomas Kelly wrote about this kind of life in his simple but profound classic, *A Testament of Devotion*. He described it as "simultaneity"—the ability to be engaged with two things at the same time:

> There is a way of ordering our mental life on more than one level at once. On one level we may be thinking, discussing, seeing, calculating, meeting all the demands of external affairs. But deep within, behind the scenes, at a profounder level, we may also be in prayer and adoration, song and worship and a gentle receptiveness to divine breathings. The secular world of today values and cultivates only the first level believing this is where the real business of mankind is done . . . But we know that the deep level of prayer is the most important thing in the world. It is at this deep level that the real business of life is determined.[26]

This certainly describes how Jesus lived. While attending to his good work of touching, teaching, healing, and helping, he was in ongoing communion with his Father—ever aware of his presence with him and in him. Times of solitude and stillness were sought and planned for, but they did not contain or constrict his communion with the Father. Instead they were times when life on two levels could be condensed to one.

Coming to see prayer as communion and not just communication changes its place in our Christian life. If God is truly our treasure, and if we have faith that through Christ we have been united with him, then prayer ceases to be a Christian's duty and becomes our joy because it is how we experience our treasure in the now.

In 1982, the *Today* show in New York City scheduled an interview with Reverend Billy Graham. When he arrived at the studio, one of the program's producers informed Graham's assistant that a private room had been set aside for the reverend for prayer before the broadcast. The assistant thanked the producer for the thoughtful gesture, but told him that Mr. Graham would not need the room. The producer was a bit shocked that a world-famous Christian leader would not wish to pray before being interviewed on live national television. Graham's assistant responded, "Mr. Graham started praying when he got up this morning, he prayed while eating breakfast, he prayed on the way over in the car, and he'll probably be praying all the way through the interview."[27]

Graham understood that his life with God was not on hold until his death. It was something to be enjoyed in the present through prayer. And while setting aside times of solitude for prayer was necessary, those minutes could not contain the fullness of his communion with God. He had learned to live all his life on two levels. On one level he engaged in the activities of the day, but on a deeper level he was in constant communion with his treasure.

7

Life *With* Faith

The Trapeze

Fear and control are the basis for all human religion. This idea was introduced in chapter 1 as we explored the nature of our existence after Eden. We live in a very dangerous world marked by chaos, ugliness, and scarcity. As we come to recognize the dangers around us, we feel afraid; and in turn we try to mitigate our fear by seeking control. We believe that through control we can protect ourselves from danger and therefore reduce our fears.

This is where religion enters the picture. In chapters 2 through 5 we saw how LIFE UNDER, OVER, FROM, and FOR GOD are each attempts at control. If you recall, LIFE UNDER GOD seeks to control the world by securing God's blessing via rituals and/or morality. What better way to control the world than by controlling the God who created it? LIFE OVER GOD takes a slightly different approach. It employs natural laws or divine principles extracted from the Bible to help us through life's challenges. Want to avoid catastrophe? Then organize your life around God's principles.

LIFE FROM GOD is primarily concerned with scarcity—not having enough. Amass enough wealth, health, and popularity and you can insulate yourself from the calamities that befall others. And all of these commodities are best acquired *from* God. LIFE FOR GOD, as depicted by the older son in Jesus' parable, tries to extract God's favor through faithful service. Accomplish enough *for* God and he will bless and protect you.

Although each uses a different approach, each of these four postures is an attempt to control the world in order to alleviate our fears—especially our fear of death. But each of them fails to deliver on this promise. In some cases they actually *increase* our fears and add to the dangers in our world. This is because our attempts at control are never enough. As finite creatures we can never acquire enough control over the cosmos to ever totally guarantee our safety. So rather than producing peace and tranquility in our souls, many forms of religion function like a treadmill with the speed gradually increasing. We run faster and faster to gain more and more control, but we never arrive at our destination. Adding to the dilemma is the fact that ensuring my safety, or the safety of my community, often requires seeking control over other people and communities. In order for me to have enough, you must have less. This leads to conflict, wars, and even more fear. The human experience might be summarized with this simple diagram:

DANGER

CONTROL

FEAR

But the LIFE WITH GOD posture departs from the other forms of religion because it accepts this simple fact: control is an illusion. No amount of control will ever be enough to ensure our safety, and no amount of control will ever remove our fears. In addition, whatever comfort we do gain through control is little more than a placebo effect. We are fooling ourselves into believing we are safe when in fact we are not. Jesus illustrated this with a story about a rich man with abundant crops (Luke 12). He built large barns to store his grain and said to himself, "Soul, you have ample goods laid up for many years; relax, eat, drink, and be merry."[1] He did not know that death would come for him that same night.

Control is an illusion, but what is the alternative? How can we be set free from fear apart from our feeble attempts at control? Henri Nouwen, a Dutch priest, professor, and author, found the answer in the Flying Rodleighs, a trapeze troupe from South Africa. While in Germany, he attended a performance out of curiosity and found himself transfixed by the artistry of the acrobats. But in the flying and spinning Nouwen saw more than an exhilarating show—he saw theology in motion.

Nouwen observed that the flyer—the person soaring through the air—is really not the star of the trapeze performance. While everyone is focused on the flyer's arial maneuvers, they sometimes fail to see that the maneuvers are only possible because the flyer fully trusts that he will be caught. Everything depends on the catcher. This led Nouwen to a new way of understanding his life with God. "I can only fly freely when I know there is a catcher to catch me," he wrote.

To more fully engage his new metaphor for the Christian life, Nouwen was fitted with a harness and ascended the trapeze himself. The sixty-something former Yale and Harvard professor giggled as he flew. And like a child, after each descent to the net, he would ask to go up again and again. Knowing he was safe allowed any fear of heights or injury to be replaced with childish joy. He said,

> If we are to take risks, to be free, in the air, in life, we have to know there's a catcher. We have to know that when we come down from it all, we're going to be caught, we're going to be safe. The great hero is the least visible. Trust the catcher.[2]

Nouwen's trapeze exemplifies faith. Faith is the opposite of seeking control. It is surrendering control. It embraces the truth that control is an illusion—we never had it and we never will. Rather than trying to overcome our fears by seeking more control, the solution offered by LIFE WITH GOD is precisely the opposite—we overcome fear by surrendering control. But surrender is only possible if we have total assurance that we are safe. We must be convinced that if we let go we will be caught. This assurance only comes when we trust that our heavenly

Father desires to be *with* us and will not let us fall.

John was the youngest of Jesus' apostles—likely just a teen-ager at the time of his calling. And when John came to the twilight of his long life, he wrote down the message that had transformed him. "This is the message we have heard from [Jesus]. . . that God is light, and in him is no darkness at all."[3] Jesus carried to earth the message of God's complete goodness toward us. God can be trusted. And this message of his good-will toward us is confirmed by the sacrifice of Jesus on the cross.

John continued: "In this the love of God was made manifest among us, that God sent his only Son into the world, so that we might live through him. In this is love, not that we have loved God but that he loved us and sent his Son to be the propitiation for our sins."[4]

It is the experiential knowledge of God's love—his unyield-ing goodness toward us—that delivers us from fear and gives us the courage to surrender to him. Real faith, real surrender is only possible in the LIFE WITH GOD posture. As John said, "Perfect love casts out fear."[5] When we live with God, when we are united with him and experience his goodness and love, fear loses its grip on our souls. With promises of God's boundless love, LIFE WITH GOD breaks the endless cycles of fear and striving for control. When we live in rich communion with God, we are set free to fly, knowing that the Catcher will never let us fall.

The Shepherd

Because more people live in urban or suburban communities than in the past, most of us fail to understand how truly stupid sheep are. Consider the news that came from Turkey in 2005. People from the town of Gevas watched in horror as one sheep jumped to its death, and then fifteen hundred others followed over the same cliff. When the villagers, whose livelihoods depended on the flock, arrived at the bottom of the mountain, they found a billowy white pile of death. Four hundred fifty sheep were lost, but amazingly one thousand animals had survived. It seems that as the pile grew higher the fall was more cushioned. It turns out the shepherds responsible for protecting the flock had left the sheep on the mountain to eat breakfast when the fleeces started to fly.[6]

The importance of a shepherd is inversely proportional to the intelligence of the animal being shepherded. Dogs, for example, manage to survive fairly well even without a human overseer. Most stray dogs have the street smarts to find food, avoid cars, and produce more dogs. Dolphins do even better; in fact, they thrive without any humans at all. Sheep, on the other hand, don't have the good sense not to jump off a cliff. They need a shepherd in order to survive.

Given the stupidity of sheep, we might be offended to discover that the Bible repeatedly compares people to the ovine idiots. But the metaphor is intended to do more than highlight our propensity to stray into danger, as legitimate as such concerns may be.[7] Sometimes sheep are threatened by forces other than their own lack of intelligence. The Scriptures affirm that we live in a dangerous world. There are wolves and famines and storms, and like sheep we need a shepherd to guide and protect us as we journey through the dark places.

In both the Old and New Testaments, God speaks of

himself as our Good Shepherd, which is meant to highlight both his benevolence and our inaneness. But where the shepherd analogy occurs in Scripture, it is usually linked to the alleviation of fear. King David, a former shepherd himself, spoke of this in one of the most familiar passages of the Bible:

> *The LORD is my shepherd; I shall not want.*
> *He makes me lie down in green pastures.*
> *He leads me beside still waters.*
> *He restores my soul.*
> *He leads me in paths of righteousness for his name's sake.*
> *Even though I walk through the valley of the shadow*
>   *of death,*
> *I will fear no evil,*
> *for you are with me;*
> *your rod and your staff,*
> *they comfort me.*[8]

The assurance that God was with him removed David's fears—even his fear of death. He knew that his shepherd would not let him go; he could release control, fly through the air, and trust that he would be caught.

Jesus picked up the shepherd metaphor: "I am the good shepherd. The good shepherd lays down his life for the sheep. He who is a hired hand and not a shepherd, who does not own the sheep, sees the wolf coming and leaves the sheep and flees . . . He flees because he is a hired hand and cares nothing for the sheep. I am the good shepherd. I know my own and my own know me."[9]

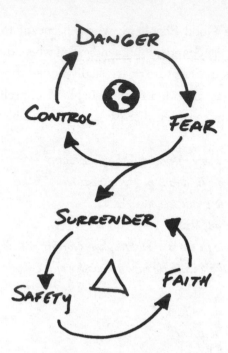

Remember that to *know* in Scripture denotes relational knowledge—an intimate relationship, and not simply cognitive knowledge. So what Jesus was describing is the same idea David expressed in Psalm 23. Knowing God, experiencing life with him, takes away our fears. Our shepherd will not leave us but will protect us from the wolves and walk with us even through the shadow of the valley of death. It is his presence *with* us that removes fear, not our ability to control him through our morality or our savviness at controlling our surroundings through the knowledge of laws or principles.

It may sound like a rudimentary idea, but God's protection over his sheep cannot be quickly glossed over on the way to deeper theologies. It is a truth that must be deeply internalized and experienced in communion with him, because it is only when we come to a profound trust in his love and care for us that our vision of the world is transformed. Rather than seeing the cosmos as a threatening place that provokes fear, with our good shepherd beside us, we can actually come to "fear no evil."

Dallas Willard observed that once we embrace the reality of God's love and care for us, we see that "this present world is a perfectly safe place for us to be."[10] Despite the dangers inherent to our post-Eden existence, if we are with God, he will see us through.

> *Fear not, for I have redeemed you;*
> *I have called you by name, you are mine.*
> *When you pass through the waters, I will be with you;*
> *and through the rivers, they shall not overwhelm you;*
> *when you walk through fire you shall not be burned,*
> *and the flame shall not consume you.*
> *For I am the LORD your God,*
> *the Holy One . . . Fear not, for I am with you.*[11]

Unlike the other four postures, LIFE WITH GOD does more than promise to manage our fears; it removes them.

But if we fail to live with God, if we opt for one of the other postures of religious life, our vision of the world will remain unchanged. Along with being perpetually stuck in the cycle of fear and control, an unaltered vision of the world means most other elements of the Christian life will fail to make sense to us as well.

Consider Jesus' most well-known teaching, the Sermon on the Mount. In this one message Jesus called us to not be angry,[12] to forgo lustful thoughts,[13] and to "not resist one who is evil. But if anyone slaps you on the right cheek, turn to him the other also."[14] He called us to give freely to anyone who asks,[15] and to love even our enemies.[16] He warned about storing up treasures on earth,[17] and the folly of worrying about having enough.[18] Despite the centrality of these teachings in Jesus' ministry, many Christians dismiss them as unrealistic.

Case in point, a few years ago I taught a class at my church about the Sermon on the Mount. On the first day, after reading the sermon aloud together, I asked the thirty adults in the class a simple question: "Do you think Jesus was serious? Do you believe he actually expects us to live the way described in this sermon?" With a show of hands, nearly everyone voted no. They did not think Jesus was serious. "Why not?" I asked.

"It's just not possible to live that way," said one woman. "No one can really love his enemy or give that generously. Jesus was exaggerating to make a point."

"It's unrealistic," another man said. "This world is going to walk all over someone who lives like that."

The comments continued along these lines for the remainder of the hour. Words like *unrealistic, impossible,* and *foolish* were frequently used to describe Jesus' teaching. The class generally believed that anyone trying to live as Jesus taught would either be miserable because of their failure to do it, or as stupid as the sheep who went over the cliff. In a dangerous world, obeying the Sermon on the Mount was tantamount to suicide.

It struck me how insistent these Christians were, most of them lifelong churchgoers, on dismissing the commands of Jesus even when he concluded the sermon by warning his listeners about the dangers of not obeying his teaching.[19] Of course, given their admiration for him, most people in the class tried to come up with some alternative interpretation for the Sermon on the Mount that didn't make Jesus look entirely detached from reality.

"Jesus was showing how it's impossible to obey God's commands. He doesn't expect us to live this way," someone added. "He was helping us see our failures and feel our need for God's grace so that we would turn to him for forgiveness."

Why is it so difficult for self-identified Christians to believe, let alone obey, what Jesus said? Well, if they still see the world as a fundamentally dangerous place in which their well-being is in constant jeopardy, then the call to love your enemy, give freely, and not worry can only be dismissed as ludicrous.

It is only when we live *with* God and come to experientially know his goodness and love that the shadows break and these commands begin to make sense. If I am eternally safe in the care of my Good Shepherd, and I come to see the world as a safe place, then I am set free from my fears. I am free to give rather than hoard. I am free to enjoy each day rather than worry. I am free to forgive others rather than retaliate against them. And I am even free to love the person determined to harm me. But all of it starts with trust (a.k.a. faith) in God's ever-present love and care for me.

The reason a great many churches and Christian ministries fail to see people obey Jesus' instructions is because the people are not living in the LIFE WITH GOD posture. The teachings and commands of the Bible may be communicated powerfully, clearly, and repeatedly, but until people have their vision of the world changed by living in communion with the Good Shepherd, until they experientially know they are *safe*, they will be incapable of following Christ's counterintuitive commands.

The Voices

On the night of January 27, 1956, Martin Luther King Jr. heard two voices. The first came when a telephone call awakened him in the middle of the night. "Listen, nigger, we tired of you and your mess. If you ain't out of this town in three days, we gonna blow your brains out and blow up your house."[20] Click.

Filled with fear, the young Baptist preacher could not sleep. Instead he poured himself a cup of coffee and sat at his kitchen table clasping his head in his hands. How had it come to this?

Two months earlier, Rosa Parks, a forty-two-year-old seamstress, had boarded a bus in Montgomery, Alabama. After three more stops the bus was filled. The driver, J. F. Blake, noticed that a white passenger was standing and ordered, "Niggers move back!" Everyone complied except for Parks. "Are you going to stand up?" Blake asked.

"No," replied Parks. She did not move from her seat until the police arrested her. The Montgomery Bus Boycott had begun.[21]

The organizers of the boycott sought the support of the black ministers in town, the youngest of whom was King at just twenty-six years old. But King was reluctant to get too involved. When invited to a meeting he replied, "Let me think on it awhile. Call me back." He eventually decided to attend, but given that the organizers had already decided to hold the gathering at King's church, he didn't have much of a choice. That was just the beginning of the surprises.

At the meeting King was quickly elected the president of the boycott committee. In truth the other leaders had "passed the buck" to the new kid in town. "It all happened so quickly,"

King recounted, "I did not even have time to think it through. If I had, I would have declined the nomination."[22]

Within days King had become the focus of the White Citizens' Council's attacks. Hate mail, obscene phone calls, threats to his wife and infant daughter came quickly. "Almost every day," he said, "someone warned me that he had overheard white men making plans to get rid of me." Then came the phone call on the night of January 27. "If you ain't out of this town in three days, we gonna blow your brains out and blow up your house."[23]

King admitted being "scared to death" and burdened by the "paralyzing effect" of fear. Over his cup of coffee he contemplated how he might leave Montgomery without appearing like a coward. "I got to the point that I couldn't take it any longer. I was weak." He confessed his fear to God as he prayed in the darkness of his kitchen. That was when he heard the second voice—an inner voice.

"Stand up for righteousness. Stand up for justice. Stand up for truth. And lo, I will be with you, even until the end of the world." The voice "promised never to leave me, never to leave me alone. No, never alone. No, never alone. He promised to never leave me, never to leave me alone."[24]

King knew the voice belonged to Jesus, and in that moment his fear disappeared. Although raised in a very religious home, theologically educated, and trained as a minister, that night in his kitchen King experienced God in a profoundly personal and intimate way. For the first time he felt the reality of God *with* him. King said the voice convinced him that "I can stand up without fear. I can face anything."

His newfound courage in God's unceasing presence would

be tested four nights later. King's wife and two-month-old daughter were home while he conducted a rally for the boycott at the First Baptist Church. As he finished speaking a church member entered and told King, "Your house has been bombed!"

When he arrived at the parsonage, King found it on fire with the front of the home destroyed. Hundreds of angry black citizens were surrounding the house with more coming from every direction. The white police officers tried to keep order, but the mob was armed with knives, bats, bottles, and guns. King made certain that his wife and daughter were unharmed and then pushed his way through the crowd to the smoldering porch.

King signaled the crowd to calm down. He reminded those who had "come to do battle" that "he who lives by the sword shall perish by the sword." Then to the amazement of both the angry black citizens and the frightened white police officers, King calmly told the mob, "I want you to love your enemies. Be good to them. Love them and let them know you love them . . . What we are doing is right. What we are doing is just. And God is with us."

One witness said there were tears on many faces. The weapons were put down and the crowd began singing "Amazing Grace." King's wife later said, "This could well have been the darkest night in Montgomery's history, but the Spirit of God was in our hearts."[25]

The sight of Reverend King, standing on the rubble of his firebombed home and calling the black citizens of Montgomery to love those responsible, changed the course of the civil rights movement. He had preached about love, forgiveness, and nonviolence before, said one historian. "But now, seeing the idea in action . . . millions were touched, if not converted."

The real conversion did not happen on King's bombed-out porch, but four nights earlier in his tranquil kitchen. There, over a cup of coffee, his fear was replaced by faith in the One who promised to always be with him.

The Sting

I know what you are thinking. *It's a nice story, but twelve years later King was assassinated. Where was the Good Shepherd's protection and safety then?* That is a fair question, and one that must be addressed if we are to be convinced that LIFE WITH GOD can take away fears and open us to genuine faith.

Martin Luther King Jr.'s courage to release control, put his faith in Jesus Christ, and love his enemies ultimately led to his murder at just thirty-nine years old. And we must not forget that Jesus, whose life incarnated the "unrealistic" teachings of his Sermon on the Mount, was utterly rejected by his own people and crucified by the ruling authorities. A little more "eye for an eye" and a bit less "turn the other cheek" might have prevented these outcomes. So far the evidence for a safe world when we seek a LIFE WITH GOD looks pretty weak. In fact, LIFE WITH GOD appears to increase pain and expedite death. Who wants that?

In order to make sense of this, we must remember two things. First, the LIFE WITH GOD posture is predicated on treasuring God above all else. (This was explored in detail in chapter 6.) It begins with the call to "love the Lord your God with all your heart and with all your soul and with all your mind."[26] If we treasure the world and a long, comfortable life in it, then we are not living *with* God. As the apostle James, known for his blunt language, said, "Friendship with the world is enmity with God."[27] So, if we are seeking God as a means of attaining status, favor, or longevity in the world, then we've missed the message of Jesus entirely.

Second, we must come to see that life for those who live with God never ends. A Roman cross or an assassin's bullet may destroy our body, but our *life*, our true self, is hidden forever with God in Christ. Jesus promised that those who belong to him would never die. They would never taste death. Of course, Jesus had a fuller understanding of death than merely the end of bodily functions or cessation of electric impulses in the brain. True death is separation from the living God, the creator and sustainer of all life, just as union with him is true life.

Eternal life, then, is unending union with God. Many people have accepted the idea that eternal life begins when their body dies, and that their present life is therefore of less importance—it is a temporary life, they believe. But if we see that union with God is promised to us today, in this present life, then our perspective changes. If we are with God, then our eternal life begins *now* and will continue forever. The life we are now living with him will never cease.

These two truths, treasuring God and eternal life with him, take away the most powerful fear we face—the fear of death. If what we treasure most can never be taken away from us, and if in our treasure is the source of life itself, then what have we to fear? In fact, it transforms physical death from the greatest fear into a moment of anticipation. It is why the apostle Paul could declare from prison, "For me to live is Christ, and to die is gain."[28] And why Dietrich Bonhoeffer, a pastor and conspirator against Adolf Hitler, could say moments before his execution by the Nazis, "This is the end—for me the beginning of life."[29]

Paul, Bonhoeffer, King, and countless others have found their treasure in Christ and walked toward death without fear, knowing they were eternally in the care of the Good Shepherd. "My sheep hear my voice, and I know them, and they follow me," Jesus said. "I give them eternal life, and they will never perish, and no one will snatch them out of my hand."[30]

Jesus not only taught this, he also modeled it. Before his arrest in the garden, Jesus completely surrendered himself to his Father. Although he knew that torture and death awaited him, Jesus prayed, "not my will, but yours be done."[31] He surrendered. He let go. He trusted that his father would catch him, that he would not be abandoned to death. After descending to the grave, on the third day he was raised up again.

The Resurrection is the means by which we have been set free from the fear of death. As N. T. Wright explained, "The point of the resurrection, despite much misunderstanding, is that death has been defeated. Resurrection is not the rede-scription of death; it is its overthrow."[32] Those who surrender themselves to God through faith in Christ partake in his resur-rection. They are granted life without end. This is why we can declare with Paul, "O death, where is your victory? O death, where is your sting?"[33]

Embracing the fact of Jesus' resurrection as we anticipate our own, we learn that placing our faith in God is a perfectly reasonable thing to do. Holding firmly to his promise to never leave us or forsake us, we can release the need to maintain a vigilant, but futile, control over our circumstance. And while others scramble every which way for safety and comfort, we can rest in the assurance of a life everlasting. Someone asked Bishop Lesslie Newbigin if he was optimistic or pessimistic about the future. He replied with the conviction of Christian faith: "I am neither pessimistic nor optimistic. Jesus Christ is risen from the dead!"[34]

The world is a dangerous place in which people fear not having enough. They toil and fight for the most basic necessities—bread, water, shelter. LIFE UNDER, OVER, FROM, and FOR GOD promise deliverance from fear and danger, but the control they offer is an illusion eventually shattered by the uncontrollable certainty of death. But those who live with God are set free from fear. Releasing control we surrender ourselves to his care knowing that our Good Shepherd will walk with us even through the shadow of the valley of death, where we will fear no evil, until we come to dwell in his house forever.

8

Life *With* Hope

The Sea

There are countless reasons why vacationers are drawn to the sea, not least of which is the immense beauty it displays. The sea is also the source of endless recreation, whether on the beach playing in the sand; on the water's surface boating, fishing, and surfing; or beneath the waves exploring the alien underwater worlds.

But for all the sea's joys and beauty, it is also an unrivaled source of destruction. On December 26, 2004, for example, the sea caused one of the deadliest natural disasters in recorded history. A massive earthquake under the sea west of Sumatra triggered a tsunami that traveled across the Indian Ocean. A wave up to one hundred feet high swept across the coastlands of fourteen countries killing 230,000 people. A similar event occurred on March 10, 2011, in Japan. An undersea earthquake triggered a tsunami that brought devastation to one of the most technologically advanced countries on earth. As of this writing, approximately 28,000 people have been listed as dead or missing.

The massive power and unpredictability of the sea is why ancient peoples saw it as a symbol of evil. The inhabitants of ancient Israel, who were not a seafaring people, viewed the ocean as a realm of chaos, destruction, and darkness. Rather than a delightful place for recreation, to them the sea was a dark abyss to be feared. In their literature, including the biblical narrative, the sea became a metaphor for the forces of evil and disorder that stood in opposition to their God of order and beauty.

The opening scene of the Bible captures this contrast. In the beginning the earth is described as "without form and void, and darkness was over the face of the deep."[1] It is an ominous and disorganized world. But then we read, "the Spirit of God was hovering over the face of the waters."[2] The God of creation brought order out of the primordial chaos. He separated sea from land, light from dark, day from night. At the end of the creation account, God declared the newly organized world "good." It was no longer a formless abyss. Instead it was beautiful and orchestrated by his good intent.

These qualities were exemplified by the garden where he placed the man and woman. Eden was the opposite of the formless sea. A garden has beauty, abundant resources, and purpose given by the gardener who cultivates it.[3] And it was God's intent for humanity, in partnership with him, to continue this ordering until all the world reflected Eden's perfection. They were to "fill the earth and subdue it,"[4] and the man began this task with God by naming the species of animals, which is to say he organized them.[5]

Sadly, the onward progress of order and beauty was severely interrupted when the man and woman broke their unity with

God. Choosing to rule without him, they plunged the world back into chaos. So now we live in a universe that does not submit to humanity's authority. We cannot control the forces around us, and the unpredictability of events means a pleasant holiday at the sea can quickly turn into chaos when a tsunami barrels ashore. Although the qualities of Eden—beauty, order, and abundance—can still be detected from time to time, they appear like the scattered remnants of a shipwreck on our world. Instead our lives are ruled by fear as we struggle to stay above the waves of a random and volatile cosmos.

But God has not abandoned his world to chaos. The biblical narrative has more to say about the sea and God's power over it. The story of the flood found in Genesis 6, which is retold in various forms throughout ancient cultures, tells of the world being destroyed by water. But the Lord preserved for himself a remnant through the deluge. Noah and the other passengers on his ark are carried safely through the chaos to dry ground.

The story of Moses also shows God's sovereign power over the sea. Pharaoh ordered all male Hebrew babies be thrown into the Nile. But Moses was put into a basket and survived the waters—a retelling of the Noah story on a micro scale. Years later God rescued his people from the oppression of Pharaoh through Moses. With the sea on one side and Egypt's army amassed on the other, the Lord separated the waters and led his people to freedom on dry land. Then, as in the story of Noah, the waters washed away those committed to evil. Pharaoh's army was no more, while those with God were preserved through the sea.

Taking these stories and others, we see that the Old Testament acknowledges the unpredictable and chaotic nature of our world as captured in the imagery of the sea and flood, but it also speaks of God's power to preserve us through it. These stories affirm that although the cosmos appears to be random, in fact it remains subject to God's purposes. His narrative will go forward and will not be thwarted by the forces of evil. Numerous psalms, influenced by the story of Israel's exodus from Egypt, speak of this fact:

> *The floods have lifted up, O LORD,*
>   *the floods have lifted up their voice;*
>   *the floods lift up their roaring.*
> *Mightier than the thunders of many waters,*
>   *mightier than the waves of the sea,*
>   *the LORD on high is mighty!*[6]

> *When the waters saw you, O God,*
>   *when the waters saw you, they were afraid;*
>   *indeed, the deep trembled.*[7]

And when King David's enemies overwhelmed him, he compared his situation to drowning in the sea. He cried for the Lord to rescue him.

> *Save me, O God!*
>   *For the waters have come up to my neck.*
> *I sink in deep mire, where there is no foothold;*
> *I have come into deep waters,*
>   *and the flood sweeps over me . . .*
> *Deliver me from sinking in the mire;*
>   *let me be delivered from my enemies*
>   *and from the deep waters.*

Let not the flood sweep over me,
or the deep swallow me up.[8]

As in the Creation account of Genesis, these stories and poems speak of God as above the waters. He is still able to bring order out of the chaos, and those united with him do not have to fear the unpredictable and powerful forces that surround them. "Fear not, for I have redeemed you; I have called you by name, you are mine. When you pass through the waters, I will be with you; and through the rivers, they shall not overwhelm you."[9]

The imagery of God's presence with his people in the raging sea may be metaphorical in the poetry of the Psalms and Isaiah, but it becomes vividly literal in the New Testament. Traveling across the Sea of Galilee, Jesus' disciples awakened him when a fierce storm came on their tiny fishing boat. "Teacher, do you not care that we are perishing?" they shouted. Jesus spoke to the sea, "Peace! Be still!" and immediately everything became calm. "Why are you so afraid?" he asked his stunned companions. "Who is this," they said among themselves, "that even wind and sea obey him?"[10]

They did not yet fully understand who was with them in the boat. In time they would come to see that he was the one who separated the sea from the land, who preserved Noah through the flood, Moses in the Nile, and led the Hebrews through the sea on dry land. He is the one before whom the waters tremble. And if he is in our boat, we need not be afraid. We will surely arrive at our destination because the forces of evil cannot overwhelm him. With God there is hope even in a world that appears to be drowning in chaos.

The biblical narrative ends with John's vision of a new heaven and a new earth. We are told in Revelation 21 that in the renewed creation "the sea was no more."[11] This observation must be read within the larger biblical context. From the opening scene of the Bible onward, the sea has been synonymous with evil and chaos. The total absence of the sea in John's vision simply means evil will have no place in the new creation. Beauty and order and abundance will fill the world, just as God had intended from the beginning.

The Anchor

Hope is the opposite of despair. When we see a random, chaotic universe, it is easy to slip into despair believing there really is no purpose, no narrative shaping our destiny. With the writer of Ecclesiastes we can shout "Meaningless! Meaningless! Everything is meaningless!"[12] Hope is the conviction that despite what we may see and experience, everything is not meaningless. There is order amid the chaos; there is a story driving all things to a culmination.

But hope is an idea that seems to have lost some of its weight. We use the word in a way that means little more than wishful thinking. "Oh, I hope the Cubs make the playoffs this year." Or it is used as a political brand making promises no candidate can possibly fulfill. But hope is much more than wishful thinking or unfounded optimism. Biblically, hope is understood to be a "sure and steadfast anchor of the soul."[13] Hope is what allows us to keep our bearing in turbulent seas; it is the assurance that the chaos we experience in this world will not win, but God's purposes will overcome. In this way hope is inexorably linked to faith. In Nouwen's trapeze metaphor, faith is the act of surrender when the flyer lets go of the bar. Hope is what the flyer experiences as he soars through the air. It is the assurance that the catcher will catch him even before he sees the catcher's hands or feels his grasp. "Now faith is the assurance of things hoped for, the conviction of things not seen."[14]

The Christian understanding of hope exists at two altitudes. First, there is the high altitude, cosmic hope that we see stretching from Genesis to Revelation in which God eradicates evil and chaos from his creation and extends order, beauty, and abundance to the ends of the earth. This larger story of hope, which is described above, can be divided into four parts.

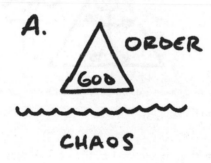

God created order from chaos at the beginning.

Humanity plunged back into chaos after rebelling against God.

CHAOS

God is present with us, providing hope amid the chaos of the world. (The stories of Noah, Moses, and Jesus calming the storm illustrate this point well.)

Evil and chaos are vanquished in the new creation.
God and his people dwell together and the sea is no more.

It is reassuring to know that the entire creation is marching forward to a day of deliverance and that the seemingly random events of history serve a greater purpose. But while this cosmic story of hope is glorious, it does not fully answer our human longing for order and purpose. What about the inconsequential events of my little life? What hope is there for *me*? What meaning and purpose can be discerned for the individual tossing and turning in the shifting seas? Our personal desire for meaning is where we discover the lower altitude understanding of hope. It is encompassed by the cosmic narrative but has its own arc; it is *our* story within the larger story.

The search for individual meaning and significance is a core struggle for many of the college students I've worked with. In chapter 5, I discussed how they often obsess about their post-graduation decisions. They want their lives to be significant, and they usually equate this with impact. But their struggle could also be understood as a desire for purpose. The college students, like the rest of us, want to believe that their lives matter—that the eighty or ninety years they may have will count for something. So they do their best to arrange their opportunities and circumstances into a coherent narrative that provides a sense of direction and meaning. They believe that hope, a sense of purpose amid chaos, is to be found through *external* arrangements that they construct.

Although the students usually operate from the LIFE FOR GOD posture, LIFE UNDER, OVER, and FROM GOD all tend to reinforce this idea. They each tell us that hope, a sense of order and purpose for our lives, is constructed externally through various means. LIFE UNDER GOD promotes moral certitude in a culture that can no longer define right and wrong. It tells us that obeying divine commands will be our anchor in these volatile times. LIFE OVER GOD, at least the non-atheist variety, says hope will come from employing God's principles in your life. You can navigate to safe harbor if you just use the right charts. LIFE FROM GOD places hope in the process of self-actualization. Purpose comes from identifying and then fulfilling one's desires. And LIFE FOR GOD finds hope in devoting one's life to the accomplishment of a purpose greater than one's self. Mission is the anchor that will give you meaning and significance.

A great many people develop their sense of direction and significance from one or more of these external constructs. *I matter because of what I am accomplishing, how morally I live, or the goals that drive me.* But can any of these withstand the forces of chaos in our world? We may build walls of morality, principles, desires, or mission to keep the sea contained, but what happens to our hope when the levies break and the world around us is swept away? Where does the athlete whose career ends because of an injury find hope? Where does the seventy-year-old whose pension was lost in a Wall Street scheme find hope? Where does the woman whose family is torn apart by divorce find hope? Where does the minister secretly struggling with an addiction find hope?

While training as a hospital chaplain in seminary, I learned that suicide was most common among the elderly. To illustrate the reason, my supervisor developed an exercise for me. On a series of note cards I wrote down things that gave my life meaning: relationships, activities, accomplishments, work, memories, etc. The thirty cards were laid out on the table in front of me as my supervisor began telling the imaginary story of my aging. First my body began to weaken. Cards with activities I enjoyed were removed. Eventually my work disappeared. Vital relationships were lost; my wife died. As the story continued fewer cards remained, even joyful memories faded away as my mind weakened. With just a few note cards left, my supervisor asked, "How would you feel if this was all that remained of your life?"

"Lost," I replied. "I would feel lost. There's nothing left. I would have no purpose."

"Now you understand why suicide begins to be appealing to the elderly," he explained. What he had really done was give me a glimpse into the despair that chaos produces.

Hope requires a sense of purpose and dignity—a belief that we matter and that our life has value. But in a world of chaos, this hope cannot come from our circumstances. Our ability to control and maintain circumstances is just too feeble. We cannot contain the unpredictable forces of this world, and putting our hope in a career, a family, a nation, or even our own moral righteousness is flirting with disaster. When they fail, and they eventually will, so will our hope. Our sense of worth and dignity gets washed away in a deluge of despair.

The Birdman

Sensing the fragility of hope, some people turn to religious institutions or communities for security. Apart from the military, they are perhaps the most skilled at instilling a sense of order and meaning to our world. For example, when tragedy strikes, people often turn to religious institutions to regain a sense of permanence and order. This may even be true of the nonreligious as we saw in the wake of the September 11, 2001, terrorist attacks or the devastation left by Hurricane Katrina in August 2005. After these tragedies many looked to faith leaders to make sense of the chaos, and they engaged religious rituals for a degree of stability in a world that seemed to have broken off its moorings.

Religion provides certitude. It defines moral boundaries, as one would expect, but many religions also assign meaning and value to certain family constructs, careers, genders, and even ages. For example, within the evangelical subculture marriage and family has taken on a predominant role, even as it declines in significance in the broader culture. Having a spouse and children gives a person identity and dignity in many churches. And as was discussed in chapter 5, many communities see a life given to Christian ministry as more meaningful than other "secular" vocations. Having a way of defining purpose, significance, and value is what many people long for in our turbulent world, and that is precisely what religion provides.

But there is an unsavory side effect. The hope that organized religion appropriates is often limited to those who conform, or conform most, to the prescribed boundaries of the faith. For example, while marriage and family is celebrated among evangelicals, a number of my single friends regularly feel devalued by a church culture that largely ignores the 50 percent of households in the United States that are not traditional nuclear families. While seeking to offer hope by cutting through the chaos of the world with clear definitions of morality, value, and significance, religious communities can unintentionally create a hierarchy that ranks a person's worth. Sadly, some who enter a religion seeking hope and significance may actually have it taken from them when they do not fit neatly within the erected boundaries. In these cases having strict order crushes hope rather than nurtures it.

The 1962 film *Birdman of Alcatraz* is the fictionalized retelling of the story of Robert Stroud, a defiant federal prisoner who kept and studied birds in his cell. Stroud, played by Burt Lancaster, refused to conform to the rigid prison system, resulting in constant friction with Warden Harvey Shoemaker. Like the injured birds he nursed back to health, Stroud believed inmates needed more space, literally and figuratively, in order to be truly rehabilitated. Symbolically, Stroud breaks open the window on the train transporting him to jail so the suffocating prisoners can breathe.

Near the end of the film, Stroud and the warden, both tired from three decades of battling each other, have this climactic exchange.

WARDEN: Not once have you ever shown a sign of rehabilitation.

STROUD: Rehabilitation. I wonder if you know what the word means. Do you?

WARDEN: Don't be insulting.

STROUD: The *Unabridged Webster's International Dictionary* says it comes from the Latin root habilis. The definition is "to invest again with dignity." Do you consider that part of your job, Harvey, to give a man back the dignity he once had? Your only interest is in how he behaves. You told me that once a long time ago and I'll never forget it. "You'll conform to our ideas of how you should behave." And you haven't retreated from that stand one inch in thirty-five years. You want your prisoners to dance out the gates like puppets on a string with rubber-stamp values impressed by you. With your sense of conformity. Your sense of behavior. Even your sense of morality. That's why you're a failure, Harvey. Because you rob prisoners of the most important thing in their lives—their individuality.[15]

This is the shortcoming of seeking hope and meaning from external conformity to a religion—it fails to truly rehabilitate us. It does not bring real dignity and significance to a person unless he or she perfectly conforms to expectations. This may help explain why increasing numbers of people are either leaving the institutional church or feeling unaccepted within it. When their lives are marked by divorce, addiction, same-sex attraction, or something else deemed "unrighteous," the dignity they long for is withheld.

Every day for nine months, Matt Russell sat at Dietrich's Coffee Shop in Houston, Texas, with a laptop, a cell phone, and a list of people who had left the church. He called everyone on the list, set up meetings, and listened to their stories. "I'd ask questions about their perceptions, their experiences, and their thoughts about church," Matt recounted. "What I heard broke my heart and changed my life."[16]

He discovered that most people had not abandoned their faith, and they had not left the church because of some doctrinal issue or change in their beliefs. Rather, most of these church dropouts were struggling with something they could not hide—abuse, sex addictions, eating disorders, gambling—any number of chronic issues. The story he heard was usually the same. They went to church, participated in the activities, got involved in a group, even confessed their sins. But over time they felt judged or unaccepted by others, so they left. The hope and dignity they were longing for never came, and in most cases neither did recovery.

What Matt Russell's interviewees needed was a form of hope that was not contingent on their morality or circumstances; one that could restore the dignity the chaos of the world had taken from them.

The Harbor

"How radical do I have to be?" the middle-aged mom asked. She had recently read a Christian book decrying the self-centered nature of much of the American church. The author had apparently had enough of the LIFE FROM GOD posture of his congregation. Instead he called readers to live a countercultural life of sacrifice and mission. The book, while inspiring, left this woman feeling "exhausted."

"I totally agreed with the book's assessment of the church. We *are* too self-centered," she explained. "But how radical is radical enough? Should I sell my house and car? Is it wrong for my kids to be attending a private school? Do I need to move overseas and work with orphans? I want to really experience the Christian life, but now I'm wondering if that's just not possible here in the suburbs."

A great many of us have come to believe that hope and significance is an external construct—something contingent on our circumstances. As a result, we fail to believe that the Christian life, at least in its fullest and most abundant form, can be lived anywhere. But as we have already seen, there are two problems with seeking hope and significance through external constructs. First, no matter how well we orchestrate our lives, we cannot prevent the raging sea, the unpredictable chaos of our world, from rushing in. Eventually what has given our lives definition and meaning will be washed away and our hope with it. And second, turning to institutional forms of religion—the kinds promoted by LIFE UNDER, FROM, and FOR GOD—for a sense of order and meaning may work for some people some of the time, but it also threatens to rob us of our dignity when we fail to conform to expectations.

But LIFE WITH GOD offers a different understanding of hope, one not rooted in either our circumstances or in moral perfection. It begins by remembering that our calling, our sense of purpose and significance, does not come from any external construct. Os Guinness said it this way: "First and foremost we are called to Someone (God), not to something (such as motherhood, politics, or teaching) or to somewhere (such as the inner city or Outer Mongolia)."[17] In other words, it is not our circumstances or behaviors or radical decisions that give our lives meaning and hope, but our unity with God himself.

The apostle Paul strongly affirmed this when writing to the confused Christians in Corinth. The Corinthians were struggling to discern what kind of life most honored God—what conditions and circumstances made a Christian life significant and meaningful. For example, was it best to be married or unmarried? Should men be circumcised (an important mark of religious identity in the ancient world) or uncircumcised? And what about work—should a slave be concerned about his or her status and seek a more noble position? Responding to their questions, Paul wrote:

> Let each person lead the life that the Lord has assigned to him, and to which God has called him. This is my rule in all the churches. Was anyone at the time of his call already circumcised? Let him not seek to remove the marks of circumcision. Was anyone at the time of his call uncircumcised? Let him not seek circumcision . . . Each one should remain in the condition in which he was called. Were you a slave when called? Do not be concerned about

it. (But if you can gain your freedom, avail yourself of the opportunity.) For he who was called in the Lord as a slave is a freedman of the Lord. Likewise he who was free when called is a slave of Christ. You were bought with a price; do not become slaves of men. So, brothers, in whatever condition each was called, there let him remain with God.[18]

Repeatedly Paul instructed the Corinthians to "remain" where they were. He said this was what he instructed in all of the churches; it was his universal message. He did not want his children in the faith falling into the deception that their significance was contingent on their circumstances. This was not to say he was opposed to changing one's marital status or career, and slaves with a chance at freedom were encouraged to seek it, but Paul did not want them to attach hope or self-worth to such changes. Instead Paul told them to remain wherever they might be "with God." What brings a person value, significance, and hope is not what he *does* but *with whom* he does it. The call to live in continual communion with God means that every person's life, no matter how mundane, is elevated to sacred heights.

Are you married? Then engage your marriage with God and learn to love your spouse as God has loved you. Are you single? Then be single with God and devote yourself to him. Are you a mechanic? Then commune with God in your work and repair cars as an act of devotion to him. Are you an office worker? Then welcome Christ to your desk as you serve your employer. Are you a homemaker? Then foster a life of ceaseless prayer, ever mindful that God is with you, amid your hectic day with your family. In other words, the fullness of Christian life can be lived anywhere, in any circumstance, because God is with us. No condition of life is more honorable than another, because nothing God does lacks value. If he is with us in marriage or singleness, and in the garage, the office, or the home, then these very different lives are each significant. Each of them carries the same dignity and hope.

This has two implications. First, it means that we do not have to upend our lives and seek a radical existence in order to have true intimacy with God. We can remain right where we are with him. If, however, in our communion with him he calls us into a new circumstance, as he did with Paul (Acts 13), we are wise to follow his leading. But the suburban mom perplexed about her far from radical life does not have to sell her home and car and relocate to an orphanage in Madagascar in order to experience the fullness of God's presence. He is perfectly content to meet her in the context of her "ordinary" life.

Second, finding our hope with God rather than in our circumstances means that if our external circumstances suddenly change, perhaps even tragically, our hope can remain intact. We can endure the storms of life that happen upon us suddenly, knowing that God is always with us. Remember, in the biblical stories of God's triumph over the sea, it was never what the people *did* that gave them hope amid the chaos, but it was God's presence *with* them. The Israelites did not rescue themselves from Egypt. God parted the sea and led them through. His presence was manifested before them as a pillar of cloud by day and of fire by night. Likewise, the disciples' seamanship did not get them through the storm. It was Jesus' presence in the boat with them that brought hope. This is why Paul drew the Corinthians' attention away from their circumstances and back to fostering a communion with God wherever they were. Hope does not depend on what's happening *around* your boat. Hope depends on who is *in* your boat.

The American church has no better testimony of hope than the one left by our sisters and brothers in Christ who endured slavery. They knew—better than most—the evil, injustice, and chaos of this world. But they found hope in knowing that God was with them in their suffering. Although many slaves attended church with their white masters, any expression of hope or prayer for freedom was strictly forbidden in these settings. One former slave described it: "Church was what they called it but all that preacher talked about was for us slaves to obey our masters and not to lie and steal. Nothing about Jesus was ever said and the overseer stood there to see the preacher talked as he wanted him to talk."[19]

But the desire for hope and communion with God was too strong for the slaves to suppress. It was not uncommon for slaves to steal away at night for secret gatherings in the thickets, swamps, or other areas where their masters were unlikely to discover them. They were known as "hush harbors"—oases where the slaves could openly express to God their longing for freedom and receive assurance of his presence with them. Often huddled on their knees and speaking in hushed tones, the slaves would hold their own worship service complete with a sermon and singing. Peter Randolph, a slave in Virginia until freed in 1847, reported that at the hush harbor "the slave forgets all his sufferings . . . exclaiming: 'Thank God, I shall not live here always!'" Another slave said, "We prayed a lot to be free and the Lord done heared us. We didn't have no song books and the Lord done give us our songs and when we sing them at night it jus' whispering so nobody hear us."[20] Many of the slaves' songs focused on the hope flowing from God's presence with them:

> *He have been wid us, Jesus,*
> *He still wid us, Jesus,*
> *He will be wid us, Jesus*
> *Be wid us to the end.*[21]

The hush harbors brought hope to the slaves at both the cosmic and individual levels. At the higher level, the slaves often compared themselves to the Israelite slaves in Egypt awaiting God's deliverance. They knew that freedom was their destiny. "I know that some day we'll be free and if we die before that time our children will live to see it."[22] At the lower level, many of the slaves found that communion with God gave them a peace and dignity that defied their circumstances. The story of a slave in Maryland known as Praying Jacob reveals this strength.

Apart from participating in whatever covert hush harbor gatherings the slaves organized, Jacob also made it his habit to pray three times each day. At regular intervals he would stop his labor, rest quietly, and enter a personal hush harbor to commune with God. This enraged his master, a cruel and terrible man named Saunders. While Jacob was kneeling in the field to pray one day, Saunders came up to him and pointed a gun at his head. Saunders ordered him to stop praying and to get back to work.

hush harbors

Jacob finished his prayer and then invited Saunders to pull the trigger. "Your loss will be my gain," he said. "I have two masters—Master Jesus in heaven, and Master Saunders on earth. I have a soul and a body; the body belongs to you, but my soul belongs to Jesus." Saunders was so shaken by Jacob's strength and lack of fear that he never touched him again.[23]

In most cases the Southern slaves were powerless to change their circumstances. Those who could reach freedom, either legally or illegally, availed themselves of the opportunity. But for the remainder, hope and dignity were not out of reach. They found both by living with God.

Most of us have far more control over the circumstances of our lives than slaves do, but like them we, too, need hush harbors to incubate our hope. We need moments to steal away from the chaos of the world in order to reconnect with the great narrative of God that promises hope for all creation. This is one of the reasons Christians gather weekly for corporate worship. In these gatherings we recalibrate our lives to the story of God in the Scriptures. We place our story in the context of his, and we remember where hope is to be found. In our songs and sharing we encourage one another with the reminder that "thank God we shall not live here always!"

But like Praying Jacob we also need to pause at regular intervals each day. We need to find the peaceful harbors of silence to pray and commune with God so that we are not overwhelmed by the chaos around us. In these moments of peace we remember that God is indeed with us, we belong to him, and that he will stay with us as we pass through the waters.

9

Life *With* Love

The Prison

Tijuana's notorious La Mesa prison contains six thousand of Mexico's worst criminals. Drug lords and murderers ferment with anger behind bars and fences, but when the tiny figure of an eighty-year-old nun appears, the men are transformed. "Mamá, mamá!" they shout as they reach their hands through the fence to touch her. Some are brought to tears at the sight of the matriarch they call Mother Antonia. "How are you, my sons?" she replies. She'll spend the afternoon praying with them, counseling them to ask their victims for forgiveness, and ensuring they have medicine and clean water. And at the end of the day, Mother Antonia will not leave the prison. She will return to the tiny cell that she has inhabited for more than thirty years alongside her "sons." "Mother Antonia brings hope to men and women here," said the warden, Francisco Jiminez. "And they find hope themselves. She spreads the love of God."[1]

Before entering La Mesa in 1977, Mother Antonia was

Mary Brenner Clarke, a blond Beverly Hills socialite, married twice, divorced twice, and the mother of seven. But at the age of forty-four, Mary's life was transformed. Her deep communion with God had resulted in an unyielding compassion for the poor and wounded. When her children were grown, she sensed God's call to serve the forgotten prisoners of Tijuana. She sold her possessions and drove across the border to take up residence at La Mesa. Mary's oldest son was not surprised by her move. "The greatest gift my siblings and I had was that our mom was on loan from God to raise us," he said. "Now she's taking care of the rest of the world."[2]

Apart from counseling the inmates, Mother Antonia became a critical link between the guards and the prisoners. She advocated for peace and humane treatment, and she reached out to the families of both the inmates and guards. The most vulnerable among the prison's population—the transvestites and the elderly—became especially close to her. One inmate said Mother Antonia is "the most important person here."[3]

Despite the remarkable transformation at the prison since Mother Antonia took up residence, La Mesa remained a very dangerous place. In September 2008, a riot broke out in the prison when she was not inside. The eighty-two-year-old arrived at La Mesa at night to find the electricity cut off and the prison surrounded by soldiers trying to contain the violence. The prisoners had taken hostages, fires had been started, and one witness said, "Bullets were flying everywhere."

Mother Antonia approached the police outside the prison. "Let me go in," she pleaded, "I know I can do something to stop the violence." The authorities refused, fearing for her safety. "I'm not afraid," she responded. "When you love, you don't have anything to be afraid of. Love casts out fear, the Bible tells us, and I love the men there . . . I can go into the cells and see the men, pray for them, bring them hope . . . That doesn't mean I'm in accord with them. That doesn't mean I'm not going to show them what's wrong and try to calm something down. It just doesn't stop me from loving them."

They let her enter. Mother Antonia entered the darkness and found an inmate named Blackie. She fell to her knees and begged him to end the riot.

"It's not right that you're locked up here, hungry and thirsty," she said. "We can take care of those things, but this isn't the way to do it. I will help you make it better. But first you have to give me the guns. I beg you to put down your weapons."

"Mother," Blackie replied, "as soon as we heard your voice we dropped the guns out of the window."

From small acts of kindness, to arbitrating the peaceful end to a riot, Mother Antonia's presence has transformed La Mesa. Sam Thompson, minister of Christian Life Fellowship in Orange, California, said, "She's a walking gift of love."[4]

The Rain

In chapters 7 and 8 we explored how the LIFE WITH GOD posture breaks the cycle of fear and control that plagues the other four postures of religious life. Once this cycle is interrupted, genuine faith (surrender) and hope (purpose) become accessible to us. But faith and hope are not the only, or the greatest, qualities to be cultivated when we live with God.

When asked about their experience with Mother Antonia,

love - genuine desire to do what is good for our enemies with + our neighbors

inmates, prison officials, and others used one word repeatedly—
love. It is the quality that marked her life more than any other.
It is also the quality Jesus said would distinguish his people. "By
this all people will know that you are my disciples, if you have
love for one another."[5] But how do our lives come to be driven
by love—a genuine desire to will what is good for our enemies
as well as for our neighbors? Where does love like Mother
Antonia's come from? How do we discover the love that leads
a Beverly Hills socialite to become the matriarch of a Tijuana
jail? Where does love that motivates an eighty-two-year-old to
walk into a prison riot come from? Where do we find a love that
is never afraid, never controlling, and never self-seeking?

Given her seemingly endless reservoir of love, it is not sur-
prising to learn that Mother Antonia began each day at 5:00
a.m. with an hour of prayer and Scripture reading. The Bible
illuminated a clear vision of God for her by driving away the
shadows of the world that seek to hide and distort our view, and
in silence she communed intimately with him. It was this time
set apart for silence and solitude that filled her reservoir of love.

○

Teresa of Avila, a sixteenth-century Christian, taught extensively
about the inner life of prayer and communion with God. She
compared it to watering a garden. Without prayer our capacity to
love will wither and die. But not all prayer nourishes our souls the
same way, just as not all forms of watering a garden are equally
effective. Teresa said the "first water" of prayer is akin to hauling
buckets from a well. We expend a great deal of energy, but it results
in very little impact. This sort of praying puts the emphasis on our

work, our words, our striving. Rather than finishing refreshed, we feel exhausted and wonder if prayer is worth the effort. Those who remain in this stage often give up on prayer entirely.

The "second water" of prayer is like attaching a rope and pulley to the bucket. The focus of prayer is still on our labor, but the work becomes a bit easier as we begin to relinquish control. Rather than filling every moment with our words and thoughts, we begin to slow down and experience moments of refreshing silence. Teresa's "third water" takes this a step further. Rather than manually watering our garden one bucket at a time, this form of prayer is like a stream irrigating the field. We become less hurried and find rest as the flow of the water does the work. Periods of silence become more common in our prayers as we entrust ourselves to God and seek only his presence rather than striving for a specific outcome.

Finally, Teresa compared the "fourth water" to rain. It is a total surrender to and union with God in which we are passive recipients of his grace. It is this kind of prayer that most effectively waters our gardens and saturates our lives with an awareness of his love. Henri Nouwen saw this kind of prayer as the beginning of ministry—the way our reservoir becomes filled with love so that we might be equipped to love others.

Why is it so important that you are with God and God alone. . . ? It's important because it's the place in which you can listen to the voice of the One who calls you the beloved. To pray is to listen to the One who calls you "my beloved daughter," "my beloved son," "my beloved child." To pray is to let that voice speak to the center of your being, to your guts, and let that voice resound in your whole being.[6]

treasuring God

Without silence and solitude with God, said Nouwen, we remain unconvinced of our worth. Instead we will live each day striving for affirmation, praise, and success. Rather than being set free to love others, we will be endlessly seeking to prove our own value. We will labor to water our gardens by drawing buckets from the world's empty wells. In the end this leads not to love, but to a dry and weary existence.

In chapter 6 we looked at what set LIFE WITH GOD apart from the other postures. It begins, if you recall, with treasuring God rather than simply seeking to use him. When God clearly reveals himself, his beauty and his goodness, he then becomes the object of our desire rather than a means of achieving some lesser goal. But in silence and solitude we discover something more: God delights in us too. We discover that we are his beloved children, and that his joy is not found in using or controlling us as instruments of his will, but rather as the objects of his love.

> The LORD your God is in your midst,
> a mighty one who will save;
> he will rejoice over you with gladness;
> he will quiet you by his love;
> he will exult over you by loud singing.[7]

In this way the LIFE WITH GOD posture begins and ends with love. God's love provokes us to treasure him, and in our treasuring we discover the joyful truth that he also treasures us. Love is the beginning and the end, the origin and culmination of our relationship with God. And along the way it provokes wonder, illuminates discoveries, and ignites joy.

○

By studying the spiritual development of children, Jerome Berryman outlined a simple but insightful pattern that I believe applies equally well to adults. When given quiet, contemplative spaces, children will more often report a sense of God's presence with them. This resulted in Berryman's first exclamation, "*ahh!*"—a sense of wonder and awe. "This sigh," he said, "suggests the presence of the nourishing mystery that feeds and yet overwhelms us with awe."[8]

As our minds with their cognitive ability catch up to the experience, there is a second exclamation, "*aha!*"—discovery. We come to recognize God more fully, and with him we discover new truths about ourselves and the world around us.

These discoveries result in joy—the exclamation of "*haha!*" Our dreary and frightening vision of the world is replaced with a joy beyond understanding. Finally, this cycle of awe, discovery, and joy compels us back into a posture of anticipation and silence so we might be with God once again.

I suspect this cycle—or some variation of it—is what Mother Antonia, Teresa of Avila, and Henri Nouwen experienced as a result of their silent communion with God. They each discovered God's delight—his gracious pronouncement that she or he was his beloved child. This in turn transformed the way they viewed themselves and others, and it produced joy even in the darkness of a Mexican prison cell. LIFE WITH GOD, in silent solitude with him, is what fuels an engine of love within us—love that is courageous, generous, and unending.

As I've shared this simple truth with others, I'm surprised

by how often I get resistance. Some people believe that before receiving God's loving presence they must "clean up their lives" in some way. One young man even told me that he continued to engage in his immoral activity in order to "get God off the hook."

"What do you mean?" I asked.

"What if I do what's right and I still don't sense God's love? What if he still doesn't bless me? That would mean there's something wrong with *him* and not just me. But if I keep sinning, then God doesn't have to love me."

"So part of why you sin is to protect your image of God?" I asked.

"I guess so," he responded. "I know it's twisted, but I'd rather be an unlovable sinner than face the possibility that God doesn't exist."

What this young man failed to realize is that even in our least lovable moments, in our rebellion and sin, God's desire is still to draw near to us and shower us with his love. After all, he is the one who makes the "sun rise on the evil and on the good, and sends rain on the just and on the unjust."[9] Even after outlining the terrible evils committed by the leaders and people of Jerusalem, Jesus nonetheless declared, "O Jerusalem, Jerusalem, the city that kills the prophets and stones those who are sent to it! How often would I have gathered your children together as a hen gathers her brood under her wings, and you would not!"[10] Such is the unrelenting love of God. His desire for us does not change even when we are immersed in sin. It is not God who rejects us, but we who resist him.

But once we experience the undeserved rain of God's love,

it sets us free from the striving for love that enslaves others. It allows us to ignore the voices of the world telling us to seek power, success, beauty, and relevance. We can put aside these voices with the confidence of knowing that we are already unconditionally loved. Nouwen continued:

> If you keep that in mind, you can deal with an enormous amount of success as well as an enormous amount of failure without losing your identity, because your identity is that you are the beloved. Long before your father and mother, your brothers and sisters, your teachers, your church, or any people touched you in a loving as well as in a wounding way—long before you were rejected by some person or praised by somebody else—that voice has been there always. "I have loved you with an everlasting love." That love is there before you were born and will be there after you die.[11]

The Greatest

First Corinthians 13 is often called the "love chapter" of the New Testament. The apostle Paul's remarks about love being patient and kind, bearing and enduring all things, seem to fit nicely with the commitments a bride and groom make on their wedding day. But the unintended side effect of linking this text so closely to marriage is that we often view 1 Corinthians 13 through the lens of modern, Western, romantic understandings of love. While Paul's words certainly have an application to marriage, Paul did not originally write them in that context.

The love chapter is the crescendo at the end of Paul's discussion of roles and gifts within the community of the church. The Corinthians had been debating which spiritual abilities were most important. Paul had talked about the ability to teach, lead, heal, encourage, and discern among others (1 Corinthians 12). While acknowledging that God has gifted people with different abilities, he debunked the Corinthians' belief that this made some people more valuable than others. And after unpacking his teaching about gifts and unity, Paul finally transitioned with: "And I will show you a still more excellent way."[12] This more excellent way is love.

> If I speak in the tongues of men and of angels, but have not love, I am a noisy gong or a clanging cymbal. And if I have prophetic powers, and understand all mysteries and all knowledge, and if I have all faith, so as to remove mountains, but have not love, I am nothing. If I give away all I have, and if I deliver up my body to be burned, but have not love, I gain nothing.[13]

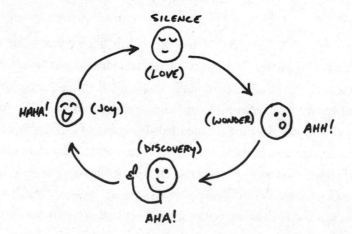

In these short verses Paul deconstructed so much of what we build our lives on. First he went after LIFE FROM GOD. He said that receiving miraculous gifts from God, the ability to speak in the tongues of men and angels, is nothing without love. Next he targeted LIFE OVER GOD. The ability to understand mysteries and possessing knowledge also cannot match the importance of love. Then he tackled LIFE UNDER GOD in the form of faith to move mountains. Finally, he dismissed even our service FOR GOD represented by our giving. None of these can benefit us without love.

How could Paul say that love is greater than gifts, knowledge, faith, and service? Because "Love never ends."[14] The qualities on which LIFE UNDER, OVER, FROM, and FOR GOD are predicated are temporary. Fear and control, which have already been seen to be illusions, will not endure. Eventually they will be undone as God restores creation to its original intended goodness. But in the renewed order, even the admirable qualities of faith and hope will cease. Therefore building our relationship with God on any of these, as the four other postures advise, will lead to great disappointment because they will not last.

Consider faith. Faith is certainly a good quality. As discussed in chapter 7, it is the courage to surrender control. But this quality is only admirable and necessary in a threatening world in which surrendering control is difficult and in which our vision of God's goodness is often obscured. But a day is coming when all dangers will be disarmed, and when God's goodness and glory will cover the earth. Then what will we need faith for? The writer of Hebrews said, "Faith is the assurance of things hoped for, the conviction of things not seen."[15]

But things will not remain unseen forever, and when the great unveiling happens, faith will be fulfilled.

The same can be said of hope. The chaos and disorder that seem to rule this world will not endure. As seen in chapter 8, in the coming age the sea will be no more; God's purposes will be fulfilled and our hope will be realized. So hope, too, will no longer be necessary.

If we return to Nouwen's trapeze analogy, we can see the transient nature of both faith and hope. *Faith* is the courage to release the trapeze trusting that the Catcher will rescue us. *Hope* is the peace and assurance we experience as we soar untethered through the air knowing the Catcher will not let us fall. But once we are caught, once we are safely and fully in his grasp, faith and hope disappear. All that remains is the love between the Catcher and the caught. "Love never ends. As for prophecies, they will pass away; as for tongues, they will cease; as for knowledge, it will pass away. For we know in part and we prophesy in part, but when the perfect comes, the partial will pass away."[16]

Paul's discourse on love is the final nail in the coffin of LIFE UNDER, OVER, FROM, and FOR GOD. These common postures, which are accepted by many and advocated by religious communities and ministries, are temporary at best. Building our connection with God on morality, knowledge, gifts, or service makes little sense in light of eternity when all of these will pass away. Even the mission of God, to which many in the church have devoted their lives, will not last forever. What will endure is our communion *with* him and the love that binds us. "So now faith, hope, and love abide, these three; but the greatest of these is love."[17]

The Stone

Throughout this book we have been searching for a way to relate to God that brings life and freedom. We all start on this journey from a common origin—our experience of a world after Eden, a world marked by fear. From this beginning we have looked at diverging paths (illustrated by the inverted mountain) that conform to five different postures. Each one promises to deliver us from fear and restore meaning, abundance, and beauty to our lives and our world, but we have seen how four of the postures fail to deliver. Only a LIFE WITH GOD sees him as our true desire rather than a device, and only a life spent in communion with him can lead us to faith, hope, and love.

But as we travel each path, we are not simply looking for a way of relating to God, we are also looking for ourselves. How we understand God and his cosmos ultimately informs how we understand our own identities.

- Am I a sinner—a despicable being, living under the constant threat of God's wrath and punishment, who must appease his will through strict obedience to moral and ritual commands (LIFE UNDER GOD)?

- Am I a manager—an autonomous being who has been given a divine manual for operating my life and world, and whose fate will ultimately rest upon how well I implement God's principles and instructions (LIFE OVER GOD)?

- Am I a consumer—a discontent being comprised of unmet desires and longings who demands all things, people, and even God to orbit around me and fulfill my expectations (LIFE FROM GOD)?

- Am I a servant—a worker created to fulfill a great mission whose sense of value is inexorably linked to what I am able to accomplish and the magnitude of my impact on the world (LIFE FOR GOD)?

At various times and in different places, each of these identities has been true of me. I am a sinner who has lived selfishly and with disregard for God and others. I am a manager who must steward resources and abilities with wisdom and foresight. I am a consumer with needs and desires that can only be satisfied by God and others. And I am a servant called by God to accomplish things in this world for his glory. Disconnected from a LIFE WITH GOD, each of these can lead to a dangerously flawed understanding of Christianity, not to mention a warped perception of God and myself. But even when tethered to a robust communion with him, none of these identities captures fully who I am.

One of the shortcomings of each of the four common postures is their inability to present an accurate vision of God. They may each reveal some part of his character, but the fullness of who he is remains hidden behind a shadow. The same is true about our identities. The identities prescribed by LIFE UNDER, OVER, FROM, and FOR GOD cannot capture the core, the essence of who I am. I am more than a sinner, a manager, a consumer, and a servant. Each may be a piece of the truth, but none reflects the entirety of my identity.

In 1 Corinthians 13, the "love chapter" explored earlier, Paul said, "For now we see in a mirror dimly." We are trying to discover who we really are, but in a world of shadows and distortion, we cannot see accurately. But the day is coming, he continued, when we will see "face to face. Now I know in part; then I shall know fully, even as I have been fully known."[18] Everything that has blocked and distorted our vision of God in this world will be gone. We will know him as fully as he knows us. And in that moment we will also discover who we truly are.

The apostle John captured this moment in Revelation 2. Speaking to his people who were struggling and persecuted, Jesus promised to give them "a white stone, with a new name written on the stone that no one knows except the one who receives it."[19] The meaning of this stone and the new name is rooted in ancient symbolism. It was customary in John's day to use small tablets, often made of wood, stone, or metal, as a token of admission. It seems Jesus was offering those who overcome a ticket into his presence and the heavenly banquet.[20]

But what about the new name? Today most names are chosen based on a parent's preference or popularity. But in the ancient world a person's name was believed to be the essence of his or her identity. George MacDonald, in his sermon "The New Name" from *Unspoken Sermons*, explained this richer understanding. He said, "The true name is the one which expresses the character, the nature, the meaning of the person who bears it. It is the man's own symbol—his soul's picture, in a word—the sign which belongs to him and no one else. Who can give a man this, his true nature? God alone. For no one but God sees what a man is."[21]

Our times in this life of silent communion with God, the moments of solitude in which we sensed his presence and love, will be a fading memory as the shadows flee and we see him face-to-face. In that moment we will possess our treasure in full, but we will possess something more as well. He will give each of us our true identity. We will also discover who we truly are; who he has created us to be. MacDonald understood that with this gift is the affirmation of our God that we had heard in silence, but then we will hear aloud. "To tell the name is to seal the success—to say 'In thee also I am well pleased.'"[22] With our new names, Christ also gives us his affirmation and love.

Identity is not something that can be fully revealed in this age, and it is not a quest that we can complete on our own. Identity is something that our Creator alone can bestow on us. As we journey through this life, we may catch glimpses of who we are—sinner, servant, manager, or consumer—but these are only broken images in a dim mirror. Our true selves cannot be discovered by living *under, over, from,* or *for* God. It is something that will only be revealed when we are fully *with* God.

There is another intriguing detail about the white stone. Jesus said that no one else would know the name written on it. It is a secret knowledge, known only to the one who receives it and the one who bestows it. Who I really am, my truest self, my most intimate identity is something that will only be shared between me and my Creator. I can only compare it to the secret knowledge shared between a husband and wife in the loving intimacy of marriage—the kind of knowledge that can be communicated across a crowded room intuitively and without words. This, I believe, is what Paul meant by "I shall know fully as I have been fully known." The love exchanged between each person and God will be so piercing and broad that nothing will be hidden from its sight.

This reality creates an intriguing paradox as we think about our eternal state of existence. John's vision reveals countless multitudes living with God in a restored cosmos; a vibrant civilization of beauty, abundance, and order filling the earth. But amid the throngs there will continue to be a secret and intensely intimate communion shared only between each individual and God. This is what we have been created for. LIFE UNDER, OVER, FROM, and FOR GOD will pass away. But our LIFE WITH GOD, like the love that fuels it, will never end.

Until then we continue to catch glimpses in a dim mirror. We continue to pursue our lives with him, find refreshment in the undeserved rain of his love, long for the day when we shall see him face-to-face, and there discover who we really are.

While imprisoned by the Nazis and awaiting execution, Dietrich Bonhoeffer composed a poem that revealed his own identity questions. Was he a pastor, a theologian, a prophet, a spy, or a conspirator? Could he be fully known by his enemies or his allies? Could he be understood by his obedience to God, his service to the church, or the content of his writings? Bonhoeffer came to this conclusion, which captures the truth for all who live with God: "Who am I? They mock me, these lonely questions of mine. Whoever I am, You know, O God, I am Yours!"[23]

Appendix A

Communing *With* God

So now what? The purpose of this book is to illuminate a different way of relating to God. In the first half I set out to reveal the popular, but ultimately unsatisfying, postures of LIFE UNDER, OVER, FROM, and FOR GOD. And in the second half of the book I sought to answer the question, What does a LIFE WITH GOD look like? We saw that it means treasuring, uniting with, and experiencing God in a way that allows faith, hope, and love to flourish in our lives.

But admittedly this book has been focused on matters of vision (*what* does a life with God look like?) rather than matters of implementation (*how* do I practice communion with God?). There is an abundance of resources spanning the history of Christianity to aid us in treasuring and experiencing Christ. Some are listed at the end of this appendix. But for those looking for an accessible start, I've included here three forms of prayer that can help move us from merely *communicating* with God toward richly *communing* with him.

Each of these practices has proven useful in my own spiritual development, and I offer them not as a prescription but merely as a recommendation. Remember, a spiritual practice is to be grasped loosely. They are each a *means* by which we commune with God and should never be seen as an end in itself. Additionally, no practice comes with a guaranteed outcome, and over time if you find a practice is not fostering your communion with God, modify or exchange it for another. This is best done in consultation with a trusted friend or mentor who can help you discern when a practice should be abandoned and when persevering may be best.

Praying with the Scriptures

Before the invention of the printing press by Gutenberg in the fifteenth century, most Christians had little or no direct access to the Bible. And even after it was widely distributed, most people were not literate enough to read it. This means that throughout most of history followers of Christ have engaged Scripture very differently than we do. As explored in chapter 3, modern people tend to approach the Bible as a manual or textbook—a document to be dissected, mastered, parsed, and implemented. In a manner of speaking, we stand *over* the text deciding what parts to read, when to read, and how to respond.

While the in-depth study of Scripture is certainly a good practice and one more Christians should engage, there is another pre-Enlightenment method of reading the Bible that is also worth practicing. *Lectio divina* (divine reading) approaches the Scriptures not as a depository of principles and applications, but as the self-revelation of God to his people. The Bible is the Living Word of God through which he still speaks and communes with us.

The practice originated in the centuries before the printing press when Christians would gather daily at the church or cathedral for the public reading of Scripture. Rather than visually reading text on the page in silence as we do, they received the word audibly as it was read aloud—a model for engaging God's Word as ancient as the Scriptures themselves. Having received and meditated on the Word of God, they disbanded as each person engaged their work for the day. But an individual would retain a word, phrase, or sentence from the Bible reading to foster communion with God in prayer throughout the day. Eventually this practice was taught in five movements.

1. **Reading.** Gently read the passage of Scripture aloud, being mindful of each word and phrase. The goal is not to read large quantities of Scripture, but to engage it reflectively and with an awareness of God's presence. This may mean reading the text multiple times. Eventually identify a word or short phrase that speaks to you in some manner.

2. **Meditating.** Having read the Scripture, in the second movement allow the Scriptures to "read you." Use the passage or phrase to guide your time of reflection and self-examination. How does the reading apply to you and your circumstances? Invite God to speak and reveal what he desires to impart to you through the text.

3. **Speaking.** After allowing God and his Scripture to have the first word, it is now time for you to respond. Communicate your thoughts to God with words. This

may be gratitude, confession, worry, joy, or any number of emotions that result from engaging the Scripture.

4. Contemplating. When speaking ceases, it is time to rest in God's presence. Use the remainder of the time to be silent and open to what God has to say. Receive his forgiveness, assurance, or whatever he may have for you.

5. Ruminating. As you conclude your time, take the special word or phrase from the reading with you. Throughout the day return to it as a prompt for prayer and as a reminder of God's presence with you.

I found the practice of divine reading particularly helpful while in seminary. The Bible had literally become my textbook, and it was difficult to read it without slipping into an academic (LIFE OVER GOD) posture. But this ancient method of engaging Scripture allowed me to once again commune with God through his Word.

Praying with the Church

In chapter 8 we learned about Praying Jacob, the slave in Maryland who interrupted his work three times daily to pause and pray. This pattern dates back to ancient Israel. The Jews set aside regular times, or "offices," for prayer in the morning, midday, and evening, utilizing the Psalms as their prayer book. Daniel practiced this routine while a captive in Babylon, and it landed him in the lion's den (Daniel 6). The tradition continued into the New Testament among Jewish Christians and later became common throughout the church.

Eventually books of Christian prayers were compiled, the most popular among Protestants being *The Book of Common Prayer*. (Complicated to use, so I suggest instead *The Divine Hours: A Manual for Prayer* by Phyllis Tickle.) The compilations include readings from the Psalms, the Old Testament, the Epistles, and the Gospels for each day, along with prayers for morning, midday, and evening. The prayers and readings are organized around the seasons of the church calendar. This meant Christians dispersed throughout the world were nonetheless united in their reading of Scripture and prayers each day.

I have found three advantages in using a prayer book and observing the offices three times a day. First, it has been a helpful step toward Paul's admonition to "pray without ceasing." It is so easy for the tasks of the day to rush at us like wild animals; in a matter of seconds we are swept up in the stampede. By stopping at regular intervals in my day, putting aside my other tasks, and spending a few minutes in Scripture and prayer, I recalibrate my mind and soul toward God rather than the things of this world.

Second, using the church's calendar and historic prayers reminds me that I cannot isolate my union with God from my union with his people. The writer of Hebrews wrote of the faithful who have preceded us as "a great cloud of witnesses" cheering us on from the stands. Using a tool like *The Book of Common Prayer* reminds me of my brothers and sisters who have prayed these same words for centuries before me. We are all connected—one household of faith, with the same God and

Father of all. Likewise, I also know that Christians throughout the world are praying and reflecting on the same words each day. This thought lifts me from the individualism that plagues our culture and many expressions of Christianity.

Finally, and perhaps most importantly, using a prayer book teaches me how to pray. Some Christians criticize written prayers as inauthentic because they are not spontaneously composed in the mind of the person praying. But when Jesus taught his disciples to pray, he offered them a preformed set of phrases—the Lord's Prayer. This wasn't because Jesus did not value authenticity or heartfelt prayers, but because he knew his followers needed more guidance.

The Lord's Prayer is like the framing of a house. It provides the basic outline and structure for how to think about God and commune with him. Without the Lord's Prayer it's unlikely any of Jesus' Jewish followers would have thought to address God as "our Father." Likewise, I am unlikely to reflect on, let alone confess, sins of omission were it not for this line from a daily prayer: "Most merciful God, we confess that we have sinned against you in thought word, and deed, by what we have done, and by what we have left undone." Written prayers guide us in our thoughts, and often teach us rich theological truth in the process. But we are still invited to adorn their framing with both the decor and decay of our lives. Rather than speedily reading over a prayer like some kind of incantation, we should allow the words to provoke our own reflections and words.

If using written prayers three times a day seems too daunting or uncomfortable, I suggest starting more simply. For example, many Christians pray before meals, and even those who shun written prayers as repetitious tend to revert back to the same clichés at the dinner table themselves. Why not use a historic written prayer, one used by Christians for centuries, to thank God for his provision? Or if you have a hectic household in the mornings, gather everyone together and read this prayer before they depart for the day:

> May the peace of the Lord Christ go with you, wherever he may send you; may he guide you through the wilderness, and protect you through the storm, may he bring you home rejoicing, at the wonders he has shown you, may he bring you home rejoicing, once again through our doors.

Sure beats "Have a nice day, kids," doesn't it?

Praying with the Holy Spirit

Socrates said, "The unexamined life is not worth living." In our busy, information-overloaded culture it is increasingly difficult to pause for self-examination. God may be present in our lives, but given the pace at which we move, it's entirely possible that we do not notice him. This is what the practice of "examen" was developed to remedy. It is a tool for both self-examination and a growing awareness of God's presence with us.

For centuries Christians have set aside a time to reflect on the events, encounters, and feelings that have filled their day. With intention they would replay the previous hours and ask themselves questions to uncover the hidden movements of God that might otherwise go unnoticed. The practice of examen often makes the most sense at the close of the day, although

I know some who begin each morning with the discipline in anticipation of the events ahead.

I suggest beginning by reviewing your calendar to bring to mind the events and activities of your completed day. As you reflect back, ask God's Spirit to reveal how he was present in each task or encounter. When were you aware of his presence, and when were you not? How might a particular activity have been different if you'd been aware of God being with you? With time this practice of reflection and daily examination will help you become more aware of God's presence during the day and not simply at the close of it.

One filter to use in examining your day involves looking for moments of what Ignatius Loyola called "consolation"—times of moving toward God. The opposite is "desolation"—times of moving away from God. What activities or moments drew you closer to God or sparked an awareness of his presence? And are there activities that regularly distract you from any sense of God? Being more aware of both of these movements can help us live with greater intentionality and aid us in developing a continual communion with him.

The practice of examen sometimes uses a series of question to uncover the deeper feelings we accumulate during the day. For example, as you play back the events of the day like a video in your mind, ask yourself, "Where was I most _____ today?" (Fill in the blank with *alive, peaceful, loved, sad, grateful,* etc.) Allow these questions to prompt prayers of thanksgiving, confession, or petition.

Many people struggle with honesty in this practice. Very often we will think back to a conversation or event from the day and dwell on how we *should* have acted or what we *ought* to have said. The goal of the examen is not to reflect on what could, should, or ought to have happened, but rather to be honest with yourself, with the Holy Spirit's help, about what *did* happen and how you *actually* felt. At times this will prompt confession of sin, but it is also an opportunity for self-examination and for God to reveal the truth about you.

In a very basic form, my wife and I also practice this discipline with our children at the dinner table. We usually go around the table and share our "highs and lows"—the high points and low points of our day. Sometimes we ask the kids, "Where did you recognize God today?" Ideally this type of simple question begins to form us to be more mindful of God during our rush of activities during the middle of the day and not simply in the tranquility at the end.

Here are a few questions to get you started with the practice of examen. Remember, these questions should be asked in communion with the Holy Spirit. Ultimately we desire him to illuminate our inner lives.

Desolation—the sense of God's absence

When, today, did I sense being drawn away from God?

When did I feel most dissatisfied and restricted today?

Was there any time today when I felt discouraged?

What was the most draining part of my day?

Was there a time today when I felt guilty, ashamed, or lonely?

Consolation—the sense of God's presence

When, today, did I feel most touched by the presence of God?

What events, relationships, or thoughts of the day drew me closer to God?

When did I feel most free today?

What was the most life-giving part of my day?

What was most joyful about my day?

Oct 20, 2012

Additional Resources on Prayer

Prayer: Finding the Heart's True Home by Richard J. Foster

Prayer: Does It Make Any Difference? by Philip Yancey

The Divine Hours: A Manual for Prayer (3 Volumes) by Phyllis Tickle

The Practice of the Presence of God by Brother Lawrence

A Testament of Devotion by Thomas R. Kelly

Eat This Book: A Conversation in the Art of Spiritual Reading by Eugene H. Peterson

Sacred Listening: Discovering the Spiritual Exercises of Ignatius Loyola by James L. Wakefield

Appendix B

Discussing *With* Others

Chapter 1—Life *After* Eden

Can you think of a time when "the coin dropped" and a different understanding of God was illuminated for you? What were the circumstances that led to this new vision?

Which of the four popular postures (LIFE OVER, UNDER, FROM, and FOR GOD) best describes how you relate to God? Has this always been the case? Can you think of seasons of your life when you related to God differently?

If you are part of a faith community or church, which posture best captures the way your community relates to God?

How do you define *sin*? How has it been taught to you in the past?

What role does fear have in your relationship with God?

Chapter 2—Life *Under* God

Can you recall a time when you tried to "bargain" with God? What was the nature of the agreement? How did it play out?

What motivates you to obey God's commands? What are you hoping to achieve? What does this reveal about your deepest desires?

Is there an explicit or implicit hierarchy of sins in your community? How can you tell when morality has slipped into moralism?

What kind of "heavy burdens" have you experienced in religious communities? Were you ever tempted into hypocrisy? How does Jesus' message set us free from this tendency?

Chapter 3—Life *Over* God

Is there an area of your life in which you rarely or never include God? What do you rely on instead?

If someone unfamiliar with Christian faith asked you, "What is the Bible?" how would you answer? What role does the Bible play in your life?

How is a relationship with God different from living out Christian values? Is it possible to live according to Scripture and not be with God? Can you think of a time in your life when this was the case?

In what ways have you reduced God to a disengaged watchmaker? Are there principles you employ as part of your faith when you ought to be communing with God instead?

Chapter 4—Life *From* God

Can you think of a way you have remade God in your own image? Can you think of something that you value highly, or a characteristic you possess, that God does not?

How have you tried to isolate yourself from discomfort? How is this encouraged by our culture or your immediate community? Do you think God always wants us to be comfortable?

If you could have all of the blessings and benefits that you desire from your faith *without* the need to pray or commune with God, would that appeal to you? What does your answer reveal about God's place in your life?

Idols are "good things turned into ultimate things." Can you think of a good thing in your life that is more important to you than God?

Chapter 5—Life *For* God

In the midst of your sins, whatever they may be, how do you think God views you?

How is the call to LIVE FOR GOD communicated in your church or faith community? What people and activities are most celebrated? What is ignored? How does it make you feel?

Are different vocations "ranked" in your community either explicitly or implicitly? How would you list them from most important to least?

In the parable of the lost sons (Luke 15), do you identify more with the younger son or the older? What truths about yourself do you see in each character?

Chapter 6—Life *With* God

Which of the five "apple cores" best represents how you have understood your religious life: divine will, laws/ principles, self, mission, or relationship? Which has been most emphasized by your community?

Would you say that you are primarily seeking to use God to achieve some other desire, or is your primary desire God himself? How can you tell the difference?

Who or what has shaped your vision of who God is? Is your understanding of God primarily positive or negative?

Can you think of a time when you had a ravishing and beautiful image of God? What contributed to this vision? What in your life clouds your vision of God?

John Piper said, "The gospel is not a way to get people to heaven; it is a way to get people to God." How were you presented the gospel? Was it bathed in fear, or in a positive desire for God?

Describe how you pray. Is your prayer life marked primarily by communication or communion? Is it a chore or a delight? What might help you engage prayer differently?

Chapter 7—Life *With* Faith

In what ways do you seek control over the unpredictable things in your life? Can you think of a situation where your desire for control resulted in conflict?

What evidence from your life confirms that control is an illusion?

What teachings of Jesus are you afraid to follow? Can you identify where your fear comes from?

Think back over the previous week. If you had fully trusted that God was with you, what might you have done differently? What "risks" might you have taken?

How are life and death redefined for those living *with* God? What significance does Jesus' resurrection have for you? Does it really influence how you live?

Chapter 8—Life *With* Hope

How does the world feel out of control right now? How does your life feel out of control? Where do you see people turning for hope?

Can you identify a time when you placed your hope in something or someone that disappointed you? What hope do you put in religion or your church?

What accomplishments provide you with a sense of purpose? Imagine each of these is taken away. How would you feel?

What is your "hush harbor"?

Chapter 9—Life *With* Love

The story of Mother Antonia shows us that love requires courage. Who do you need more courage to love? What does Mother Antonia's example tell us about how to find this courage?

Henri Nouwen wrote about God's voice speaking to our center, and Zephaniah said God exults over us with singing. What do you think God sings over you?

Why is love more important than faith or hope? Which is more evident and emphasized in your faith community?

What names, good and bad, have you been called that have shaped your identity? Anticipating the day when Jesus will give you a white stone with a new name on it, what do you think the name might be? What name captures how God sees you?

Notes

Chapter 1

1. Tatyana Tolstaya, "See the Other Side," trans. Jamey Gambrell, *New Yorker*, March 12, 2007.
2. G. K. Chesterton, *What's Wrong With the World* (Boston: Adamant Media, 2004), 48.
3. Skye Jethani, *The Divine Commodity: Discovering a Faith Beyond Consumer Christianity* (Grand Rapids: Zondervan, 2009).
4. John 13:35.
5. John 1:1–2 ESV.
6. Genesis 1:26 ESV.
7. Genesis 2.
8. Genesis 1:28 ESV.
9. Revelation 21:2–3 ESV.
10. Revelation 5:9–10 ESV.
11. Revelation 22:5 ESV.
12. Genesis 3:4–6 ESV.

Chapter 2

1. Steve Johnson quoted in Sean Brennan, "Bills receiver Steve Johnson appears to blame God in tweet for awful dropped pass against Steelers," *NY Daily News*, November 29, 2010, http://articles.nydailynews.com/2010-11-29/sports/27082588_1_tweet-steelers-fan-falcons (accessed May 30, 2011).
2. Cicero, *De Natura Deorum*, 3.89.

3. Matt Chandler, "Preaching the Gospel to the De-Churched" (lecture, Advance 09, Durham, North Carolina, June 4, 2009).

4. Deuteronomy 5:16 ESV.

5. "Hamas bans men from working in women's hairdressers," *The Telegraph*, March 5, 2010, http://www.telegraph.co.uk/news/worldnews/middleeast/palestinianauthority/7371960/Hamas-bans-men-from- working-in-womens-hairdressers.html (accessed May 30, 2011).

6. "Jihad Against Jews and Crusaders," *World Islamic Front Statement*, February 23, 1998, http://www.fas.org/irp/world/para/docs/980223-fatwa.htm (accessed May 30, 2011).

7. Jerry Falwell quoted in "Falwell apologizes to gays, feminists, lesbians," *CNN*, September 14, 2001, http://archives.cnn.com/2001/US/19/14/Falwell.apology.html (accessed May 30, 2011).

8. Charmaine Noronha, "Tony Blair, Christopher Hitchens Debate Religion," *The Huffington Post*, November 27, 2010, http://www.huffingtonpost.com/2011/11/27/tony-blair-christopher-hi_n_788717.html (accessed May 30, 2011).

9. John 9:2–3 ESV.

10. Luke 18:24–25 NIV.

11. Matthew 23:4 ESV.

12. Matthew 11:28–30 ESV.

13. Matthew 23:23 ESV.

14. Matthew 23:25.

15. Matthew 23:27 ESV.

16. Luke 5:30 ESV.

17. Isaiah 29:13 NIV; Matthew 15:8–9.

Chapter 3

1. "500 Greatest Songs of All Time," *Rolling Stone*, April 7, 2011, http:// http://www.rollingstone.com/music/lists/the-500-greatest-songs-of-all-time-20110407/john-lennon-imagine-19691231 (accessed May 30, 2011).

2. Mitchell Landsberg, "Religious skeptics disagree on how

aggressively to challenge the devout," *Los Angeles Times*, October 10, 2010.

3. Landsberg, "Religious skeptics."

4. Václav Havel quoted in Timothy Garton Ash, "The Truth about Dictatorship," *New York Times Review of Books*, February 19, 1998, 36–37.

5. Stéphane Courtois et al., *The Black Book of Communism: Crimes, Terror, Repression*, trans. by Jonathan Murphy and Mark Kramer, ed. by Mark Kramer (Cambridge, MA: Harvard University Press, 1999), 4.

6. Pew Forum on Religion and Public Life, *U.S. Religious Landscape Survey* (Washington: Pew, 2008), 5, http://religions.pewforum.org/pdf/report-religious-landscape-study-full.pdf (accessed May 30, 2011).

7. Associated Press, "Many who pledge abstinence at risk for STDs," *MSNBC.com*, March 18, 2005, http://www.msnbc.msn.com/id/7232643/ns/health-sexual_health/t/many-who-pledge-abstinence-risk-stds/ (accessed May 30, 2011).

8. Andy Stanley quoted in "Leader's Insight: Get-It-Done Leadership," *Leadership Journal*, Spring 2006, http://www.christianitytoday.com/le/currenttrendscolumns/leadership-weekly/cln70528.html (accessed May 30, 2011).

9. John 5:39–40 ESV.

10. Laurie Beth Jones, *Jesus, CEO: Using Ancient Wisdom for Visionary Leadership* (New York: Hyperion, 1995), xvii.

11. Barna Group, "Church Priorities for 2005 Vary Considerably," *Barna Update*, February 14, 2005, http://www.barna.org/barna-update/article/5-barna-update/185-church-priorities-for-2005-vary-considerably?q=prayer (accessed May 30, 2011).

12. Exodus 17:1–7.

13. Numbers 20:8 ESV.

14. Group Publishing, "HOW 2 Children's Ministry Conference," Facebook, http://www.facebook.com/event.php?eid=36623289035&index=1 (accessed May 30, 2011).

15. A search of the "Christian" book category on Amazon found

nearly 2,000 books with the word *principles* in the title and 500 with the word *effective*.

16. Michael Horton, "All Crossed Up," *Touchstone: A Journal of Mere Christianity*, March 2008, http://www.touchstonemag. com/archives/article.php?id=21-02-011-v (accessed May 30, 2001).

17. Numbers 20:11 ESV.

Chapter 4

1. Scot McKnight, *The Blue Parakeet* (Grand Rapids: Zondervan, 2009), 220–223.

2. McKnight, *Blue Parakeet*, 49.

3. François-Marie Voltaire quoted in Isaac Everett, *The Emergent Psalter* (New York: Church Publishing, 2009), 108.

4. Christian Smith, *Soul Searching: The Religious and Spiritual Lives of American Teenagers* (New York: Oxford University, 2005), 165.

5. Christian Smith quoted in Tony Jones, "Youth and Religion: An Interview with Christian Smith," 2005, Youth Specialties, http://www.youthspecialties.com/articles/youth-and-religion-an-interview-with-christian-smith (accessed May 30, 2011).

6. Isaiah 42:5.

7. James 1:17 ESV.

8. Luke 11:11–13.

9. Joyce Meyer quoted in David Van Biema and Jeff Chu, "Does God Want You to Be Rich?" *Time*, September 10, 2006.

10. Robert Paul Reyes, "Joyce Meyer's $23,000 Toilet: A Symbol of the Prosperity Gospel," *American Chronicle*, November 9, 2007.

11. Rodney Clapp, "Why the Devil Takes VISA," *Christianity Today*, October 7, 1996.

12. John De Graff, ed., *Take Back Your Time* (San Francisco: Berrett-Koehler, 2003), 95.

13. Kevin Bales, *Disposable People: New Slavery in the Global Economy* (Berkeley: University of California, 1999), 8.

14. Neil Postman, *Amusing Ourselves to Death: Public Discourse in the Age of Show Business* (New York: Viking Penguin, 1985).
15. Isaiah 22:13 ESV; 1 Corinthians 15:32 ESV.
16. C. S. Lewis, *The Problem of Pain* (New York: Macmillan, 1944), 81.
17. Paul W. Brand and Philip Yancey, *The Gift Nobody Wants* (New York: HarperPerennial, 1995).
18. Deuteronomy 8:11–14 ESV.
19. Isaiah 29:13 ESV.
20. Leviticus 20:9.
21. Luke 15:13 ESV.
22. Timothy Keller, *Counterfeit Gods: The Empty Promises of Money, Sex, and Power and the Only Hope that Matters* (New York: Dutton, 2009).
23. Matthew 10:37 ESV.
24. Matthew 6:19–24.
25. Luke 9:58.
26. Matthew 6:1–4.
27. Courtney Hutchison, "Today's Teens More Anxious, Depressed, and Paranoid Than Ever," *ABC News*, December 10, 2009.
28. Jean Twenge quoted in Hutchison, "Today's Teens."
29. Cathy Lynn Grossman, "Young adults aren't sticking with church," *USA Today*, August 6, 2007.
30. Luke 15:14–19.
31. Luke 15:20 ESV.
32. Luke 15:21–24.

Chapter 5

1. Acts 13:1–2.
2. Ephesians 3:1 ESV.
3. 1 Corinthians 9:22–23 ESV.
4. Philippians 3:8–9 ESV.
5. 1 Thessalonians 4:11 NIV.
6. Ephesians 3:14–19 ESV.
7. Matthew 7:22–23 ESV.
8. Gordon MacDonald, "Dangers of Missionalism," *Leadership*

Journal, January 1, 2007 http://www.christianitytoday.com/le/2007/winter/16.38.html (accessed May 31, 2011).

9. Phil Vischer, *Me, Myself, and Bob* (Nashville: Thomas Nelson, 2007), 238.

10. Vischer, *Me, Myself, and Bob*, 237.

11. MacDonald, "Dangers of Missionalism."

12. Horton, "All Crossed Up."

13. Dave Johnson quoted in "Leader's Insight: The High Price of Dying (to Self)," *Leadership Journal*, April 16, 2007, http://www.christianitytoday.com/le/currenttrendscolumns/leadershipweekly/cln70416.html (accessed May 31, 2011).

14. Luke 15:11–32.

15. Luke 15:29–30 ESV.

16. Luke 15:31–32 ESV.

Chapter 6

1. Brother Lawrence, "Fifth Letter," *The Practice of the Presence of God the best rule of a Holy Life*, trans. Joseph de Beaufort (New York: Fleming H. Revell, 1895), 32.

2. "Letter 89," *The Letters of J. R .R. Tolkien*, ed. Humphrey Carpenter (Boston: Mariner, 2000), 99–100.

3. John 1:1–2 ESV.

4. I recommend Robert Letham's work *The Holy Trinity in Scripture, History, Theology, and Worship* (Phillipsburg: P&R Publishing, 2005).

5. Kevin DeYoung, "The Most Important Doctrine Many Never Think About," *The Gospel Coalition Blog*, September 22, 2009, http://thegospelcoalition.org/blogs/kevindeyoung/2009/09/22/most-important-doctrine-many-never/ (accessed May 31, 2011).

6. Mark 5:15, 17–18 ESV.

7. Colossians 1:15 ESV.

8. Matthew 13:44–46 ESV.

9. Isaiah 53:6 ESV.

10. John 1:29 ESV.

11. Mark 10:45 ESV.

12. Isaiah 53:6 ESV.
13. John Piper, *God Is the Gospel* (Wheaton: Crossway, 2005), 47.
14. Revelation 21:3 ESV.
15. 1 Corinthians 13:12 NIV.
16. Philippians 3:8; Galatians 4:9; 1 John 4:8.
17. Dallas Willard, *The Divine Conspiracy* (Wheaton: HarperCollins, 1997), 428.
18. Luke 11:1 ESV.
19. Matthew 6:9–13; Luke 11:2–4.
20. John 5:19 ESV.
21. John 14:10–11 ESV.
22. Mother Teresa, quoted in Chuck Swindoll, *So You Want to Be Like Christ? Eight Essentials to Get You There* (Nashville: Thomas Nelson, 2005), 61–62.
23. 1 Thessalonians 5:17 ESV.
24. John 14:20 ESV.
25. John 15:4–5 ESV.
26. Thomas R. Kelly, *A Testament of Devotion* (New York: HarperCollins, 1992), 9.
27. T. W. Wilson quoted in Harold Myra and Marshall Shelley, *The Leadership Secrets of Billy Graham* (Grand Rapids: Zondervan, 2005).

Chapter 7

1. Luke 11:19 ESV.
2. Henri Nouwen quoted in *Angels over the Net*, DVD, directed by The Company (New York: Spark Productions, 1995).
3. 1 John 1:5 ESV.
4. 1 John 4:9–10 ESV.
5. 1 John 4:18 ESV.
6. "450 sheep jump to their deaths in Turkey," *USA Today*, July 8, 2005.
7. Isaiah 53:6.
8. Psalm 23:1–4 ESV.
9. John 10:11–14 ESV.
10. Willard, *The Divine Conspiracy*, 208.

11. Isaiah 43:1–5 ESV.
12. Matthew 5:21–22.
13. Matthew 5:27–28.
14. Matthew 5:39 ESV.
15. Matthew 5:42.
16. Matthew 5:44.
17. Matthew 6:19.
18. Matthew 6:31.
19. Matthew 7:26–27.
20. Harvard Sitkoff, *King: Pilgrimage to the Mountaintop* (New York: Hill and Wang, 2007), 38.
21. Sitkoff, *King*, 23.
22. Ibid., 28–30.
23. Ibid., 38.
24. Ibid.
25. Ibid., 37–39.
26. Matthew 22:37 ESV.
27. James 4:4 ESV.
28. Philippians 1:21 ESV.
29. Dietrich Bonhoeffer, *Life Together* (New York: HarperCollins, 1954), 13.
30. John 10:27–28 ESV.
31. Matthew 26:39 ESV.
32. N. T. Wright, *Surprised by Hope* (New York: HarperOne, 2008), 50.
33. 1 Corinthians 15:55 (ESV).
34. Lesslie Newbigin quoted in N. T. Wright, *Surprised by Hope*, 108.

Chapter 8

1. Genesis 1:2 ESV.
2. Ibid.
3. Genesis 2:9.
4. Genesis 1:28 ESV.
5. Genesis 2:19–20.
6. Psalm 93:3–4 ESV.

7. Psalm 77:16 ESV.
8. Psalm 69:1–2; 14–15 ESV.
9. Isaiah 43:1–2 ESV.
10. Mark 4:35–41 ESV.
11. Revelation 21:1 ESV.
12. Ecclesiastes 1:2 NIV.
13. Hebrews 6:19 ESV.
14. Hebrews 11:1 ESV.
15. *Birdman of Alcatraz*, DVD, directed by John Frankenheimer (1962; Century City, CA: MGM, 2001).
16. Matt Russell and Angie Ward, "Can Your Church Handle the Truth?" *Leadership Journal*, July 13, 2009, http://www.christianitytoday.com/le/communitylife/discipleship/canyourchurchhandle.html (accessed May 31, 2011).
17. Os Guinness, *The Call: Finding and Fulfilling the Central Purpose of Your Life* (Nashville: Thomas Nelson, 1998), 31.
18. 1 Corinthians 7:17–18; 20–24 ESV.
19. Albert J. Raboteau, *Slave Religion: The "Invisible Institution" in the Antebellum South* (New York: Oxford Press, 1978), 213–214.
20. Raboteau, *Slave Religion*, 217–218.
21. Ibid., 211.
22. Ibid., 219.
23. Ibid., 306.

Chapter 9

1. Johnny Dodd, "From Beverly Hills to Mexican Jail," *People* 63, no. 20 (May 23, 2005): http://www.people.com/people/archive/article/0,,20147637,00.html (accessed May 31, 2011).
2. Ibid.
3. Ibid.
4. Ibid.
5. John 13:35 ESV.
6. Henri Nouwen, "Moving from Solitude to Community to Ministry," *Leadership Journal*, Spring 1995, http://www.

christianitytoday.com/le/1995/spring/51280.html (accessed May 31, 2011). Used with permission.

7. Zephaniah 3:17 (ESV).

8. Jerome W. Berryman, *Godly Play: An Imaginative Approach to Religious Education* (San Francisco: Harper, 1991), 150.

9. Matthew 5:45 ESV.

10. Luke 13:34 ESV.

11. Nouwen, "Moving from Solitude."

12. 1 Corinthians 12:31 ESV.

13. 1 Corinthians 13:1–3 ESV.

14. 1 Corinthians 13:8 ESV.

15. Hebrews 11:1 ESV.

16. 1 Corinthians 13:8–10 ESV.

17. 1 Corinthians 13:13 ESV.

18. 1 Corinthians 13:12 ESV.

19. Revelation 2:17 ESV.

20. Robert H. Mounce, *What Are We Waiting For? A Commentary on Revelation* (Eugene: Wipf and Stock, 1992), 10.

21. George MacDonald, *Unspoken Sermons* (New York: Cosimo Classics, 2007), 55.

22. MacDonald, *Unspoken Sermons*, 57.

23. Dietrich Bonhoeffer, *Letters and Papers from Prison* (New York: MacMillan), 348.

Acknowledgments

Dave Schreier has been an indispensable friend for nearly two decades. We've walked through every posture of relating to God, and together discovered the blessed simplicity of a life with Christ. His encouragement, belief in my calling, and commitment to live with God contributed to every part of this book.

My writing partners, Andy Brumbach and Dan Haase, endured countless drafts and outlines as I processed the ideas of this book. Their artistic sensibilities and empathy as writers were invaluable during the months of labor. I'm particularly indebted to Dan for convincing me to drop other ideas and focus on writing *With*.

Joel Miller and his team at Thomas Nelson saw the potential in this book very early. His objective feedback and editor's scalpel has made this a better work than it otherwise would have been.

Kathy Helmers and the crew at Creative Trust helped me take this project from idea to reality. Thanks for taking a chance on a young voice with something to say.

Brian and Cheryl Baird, Dave and Mary Conner, Scottie May, Bob and Cindy Rinaldi, and Tom and Mary Ellen Slefinger were instrumental in crafting the group discussion questions in the appendix. Their feedback on the book's content also led to revisions and a stronger, clearer message. I've also been blessed by their friendship and authenticity.

Although they remain nameless throughout the book, I must recognize the college students I've engaged with over the last five years. Their honesty about their struggles, combined with a genuine desire to know God, was the spark for this book. My wife Amanda has shown immense patience and resilience during the season of transition in which I wrote *With*. My love and appreciation for her is written with invisible ink on every page of this book.

About the Author

Skye Jethani is the managing editor of Leadership Journal, a publication of Christianity Today International. Skye also contributes regularly to Catalyst Leadership, Relevant, and The Huffington Post. Skye's blog, SKYEBOX, was awarded second prize for the best Christian blog by the Evangelical Press Association.

Skye has been featured in newspapers around the country and is a frequent speaker at ministry conferences such as Catalyst, Q, and Moody Pastor's Conference.

Skye earned a Masters of Divinity degree in 2001 from Trinity Evangelical Divinity School in Deerfield, Illinois. He and his wife, Amanda, currently live in Wheaton, Illinois, with their three children Zoe, Isaac, and Lucy.